MY LIFE:
WHAT WILL I
MAKE OF IT?

MY LIFE:
WHAT WILL I
MAKE OF IT?

By

ROWENA FERGUSON

Rand McNally & Company

Chicago · New York · San Francisco

For Mary Proudfoot Ferguson

CONTENTS

MY LIFE:
WHAT WILL I
MAKE OF IT?

ASKING IMPORTANT QUESTIONS

PEOPLE are always asking questions. Children ask them, young people ask them, and adults ask them. Young students ask questions and the greatest scientists continue to ask them. To some questions answers are found easily and quickly; to others the answers are found only by long and hard searching. Finding the answers to questions is an important way people learn about themselves, about other people, about life, about the world, about the way things are and why.

People ask questions because they are curious to know facts about themselves and the world they live in. They ask questions also because they are interested in meanings. That is, they search not only for the facts about their world but also for the significance of those facts. What is their meaning; what truth do they point to? Another reason people ask questions is because they want to clear up uncertainty. They wish to be sure of things, to know what really is and what is not. Still another reason for questions is concern for the future. People wonder and sometimes worry about what the future will be like. If I do thus and so, they ask, what is likely to happen?

When people begin to find answers to such questions, they can make plans for the future—not, of course, with absolute certainty. But they can plan with much more confidence, and often with such a reasonable degree of certainty that they can venture to act for the future.

The value of asking questions, therefore, is that seeking answers enables people to get a fairly accurate picture of themselves and of other people, to understand the world they live in. This gives them a basis of security from which to launch plans for the future and to carry on confidently.

Some of the questions people ask are basic to most other questions. In fact, until a person has dealt with these basic questions he finds it hard to arrive at reliable answers to most of his other questions. This book is about some of these basic questions. We have selected six questions that people ask about themselves and we have phrased them this way: Where Did I Come From? Who Am I? What Am I Here For? What Will I Become? What Will My Life Be Like? Where Do I Fit In?

These are questions which most young people are curious about, although they may word them differently, or they may not put their wonderment into words at all. These questions are treated in this book from the viewpoint of a young period of life, but the same questions are pertinent at every period.

To raise a question is to hope for an answer. This book is going to suggest some ways of answering these particular questions which many people today, and many more people during the long past, have found to be true, reliable, and satisfying. But let's say right away that they are not intended to be *your* answers. Out of your experience plus your thoughts and feelings about those experiences you will build your own answers. No one does this building all by himself, of course; he gets help from many sources, and so will you. This book is one of these sources to help you find your own answers; the answers which are real and true for you.

First, let us think about how people go about finding their answers to such questions. Where do the answers come from? In general, they come from man's experiences through several broad fields of thought and investigation. For example, through science, religion, history.

Science has to do with findings about the world and about people which can be picked up by our five senses, or learned through experiment in a laboratory, or observation through a telescope, or in similar ways. The scientist reflects upon, manipulates, analyzes, and generalizes about these findings. He thus produces some answers which can be demonstrated at that time to be factual, or reasonably presumed to be so. Such scientific effort is organized into several fields—mathematics, chemistry, geology, biology, physics, sociology, psychology, anthropology.

Religion has to do with meanings and values in life. It suggests answers in terms of "why" something is. It seeks answers about human happiness and goodness. It seeks answers about ultimate reality—that is, the fundamental truths about the purpose of living and the destiny of people. These findings of religion are not open to proof by scientific methods. Instead, they are what we call matters of faith. This does not mean that seeking answers from religious faith is believing something that is not so. Rather, it means that religious faith offers answers that are found to be true in a way different from the way of science. They are not tested in a scientific laboratory; they are tested in the lives of persons. That is, they have enabled persons to be courageous in difficulties, generous and helpful in responding to others, and happy and creative in spite of handicaps. Thus, they have actually been verified in the lives of many groups and many individual persons.

These two sets of findings from science and from religion are not in conflict with each other. Each one looks at the world and people from a particular viewpoint, and what each one says about the world may be equally true. For example, we may say with the scientists that the moon revolves around the earth, and that the earth and the other planets revolve around the sun, and that our solar system is only one of a vast number in the universe. This is true. At the same time we may say with the psalmist, "The heavens declare the glory of God." This also is true. The scientific statement represents facts which men have discovered by investigation; the religious statement represents

14

man's faith that what has been discovered bears witness to purpose, to the Creator, God. The truth discovered through faith is as valid as is the truth discovered through a scientific method.

A well-rounded view of life must take account of both kinds of findings. Religion must accept facts of scientific discovery about the movements and physical characteristics of the planets and allow for them in shaping the affirmations of faith about the nature of the universe. Similarly, science must recognize that it does not have the only or the whole truth about the solar system; it must allow for findings from faith that our solar system is part of an infinite design which has beauty and meaning.

At the same time, in searching for answers to important questions we need to consider *history*, which represents the accumulation of the experience of the human family from long ago to now. Part of this experience is recorded in the Bible; part of it in history since Bible times; part of it in the history of only yesterday. As we reflect upon this accumulated experience, we may gain understanding of what makes for human misery and what makes for human happiness, in both individual and national life.

Persons asking questions about the world and about life must bring these different viewpoints into a relationship with each other that is orderly and convincing. This is what we are trying to do in this book. In considering the important questions most people ask, we shall bear in mind the findings of science and religion and human history. But because in your schoolwork you are considering all the time the findings of science and history, our focus in this book will be on matters of religion. Thus the content of each chapter will be drawn largely from the truth about persons and life in our world which is affirmed by faith through the Judeo-Christian tradition. This tradition is not only truth from the past. It includes truths that are verified in the experience of persons today.

In this perspective, let's consider these important questions.

1.

WHERE DID I COME FROM?

THERE is an answer to the first question—Where did I come from?—that at first glance seems very simple. You come from God. But immediately we want to know: How can this be? What does it mean? And then the answer gets more complicated. It also gets rich in meaning and exciting in its implications.

YOU COME FROM GOD

To say "You come from God" is an answer in faith. We do not try to prove it by scientific methods. Rather we affirm it because as men live their lives in the world it seems to them to be the true answer.

To think of ourselves with minds and bodies, to think of a galaxy in the remote heavens or a single star like the red giant, Antares; or the green reach of a wheat field blowing in the wind; or a flower like a yellow daffodil; or a quartz crystal or a snowflake with their orderly structures—to call to mind this created world brings an inner feeling of confidence that it did not all just happen to be. We experience the reality, order, beauty, and purpose which to us bear witness to its Creator.

We therefore say, "You come from God" because of our faith that back of, and beyond, and in all that exists is the Creator. In the beginning there is God. It was God's will, purpose, and creative act which brought into being all that we know: the physical universe with its tremendous reaches of space and variety of forms, and all living things, including humankind.

This faith and this mood were reflected long ago by the writers of the first chapters of the book of Genesis in the Bible; they are experienced today by persons all around the world.

YOU WERE BORN INTO GOD'S WORLD

To say that our world is created by God does not deal with the question of *how* it was created. It does affirm that it did not come into being by accident, that it is not arbitrary and nonsensical. The fact is that the created world, in its whole and in its parts, adds up; thoughtful persons can make sense of it. A large part of the work of scientists is doing just that: making sense of the created world.

Another way of saying this is to say that the created

world yields to investigation. Scientists have learned to explore the long history of creation, to observe and describe the physical universe as it now is. Often they can predict its processes in reliable and reasonable terms: for example, the timing and orbits of comets, the occurrence of an eclipse of the sun, the approach of a snow storm, the path of a hurricane. The present age of space exploration is possible because the universe is predictable. That is, it is orderly in its processes. Because its laws can be understood and used, the orbit of a space vehicle can be plotted accurately. Indeed, our everyday lives depend upon this fact of predictability. Our food, clothing, and health rest upon the orderly procession of the seasons and the processes that make possible the sciences of agriculture, biology, and chemistry.

This does not mean that the universe is a vast machine which we can master and manipulate mechanically. For all man's discoveries about the physical world, he is not yet the master of it, and he may never be able to predict everything about it and control it. Man's understanding is limited. He is a creature, not God. But men do know enough to realize that natural objects, events, and processes are not mechanical in their orderliness; they seem rather to run according to some dynamic principle. That is, they seem to run according to a principle involving change and development and purpose rather than by either meaningless chance or machinelike rigidity. An interesting evidence of this principle is the recent discovery through radio-astronomy of some celestial objects not observed be-

19

fore. They are unlike anything the scientists have known about and are now called "quasars," which means they display some but not all the characteristics of stars. They seem not to be really stars, but what they are and how they are related to other bodies in space is still being investigated.

People have always recognized that they are dependent on physical resources and processes, and have been interested in the natural world as the setting for human life. The ancient Hebrews who put together and wrote down the early chapters of Genesis thousands of years ago were influenced by these concerns. They expressed wonder and awe when they thought about the created world, and asked the question: Where did everything, including me, come from? These people, however, lived in a prescientific era; they did not possess the technology to explore and describe the universe and its beginnings in scientific terms. In fact, these early men did not think nor write from a scientific point of view at all. They thought and wrote from the viewpoint of religious faith. In those terms, using poetic imagery, they described God's activity in creation: "In the beginning God created the heavens and the earth." Thus they affirmed the most important aspect of our faith about the created world: that God planned it and has a purpose for it. This basic understanding is as sound today as it was in long-ago Palestine. Indeed, we believe this is why the scientists find the world predictable, why they can explore it, and gradually can come to understand it.

LEARNING ABOUT GOD'S WORLD

Modern science can tell us a great deal about what the physical universe is like and something about how it may have come into existence. Scientists have used their minds and imaginations to probe the mysteries of nature. Their discoveries tend to underline the beauty, complexity, and meaningfulness of the natural order. Thus, the more men discover about the created world the more strongly it bears witness to its Creator, his nature, power, wisdom, and purpose. And man's joy in discovering and understanding bears witness to the goodness of God in enabling man to think and explore and plan and share responsibility.

Just as people learn more and more in scientific investigation, they learn more and more in the exploration of religious faith. Several generations ago some people had the idea that they could understand the Bible without taking into account the life and times out of which various parts of the Bible came to us, nor the apparent literary forms of its writings. Many of these same people had a very dim understanding of what science is and what it tries to do. Out of this situation, a conflict arose between some persons representing science and some representing a religious tradition based on the Scriptures. In the popular mind, science and religion were seen to be at odds: you had to choose one or the other. In this conflict of arguments, both some men of science and some men of religion were mistaken.

These mistaken notions about both science and religion

and the relation between them belong to the past. Today we recognize that science and religion represent two ways of looking at the same thing which may support each other, and together help us know more of the truth about our world. Science describes process, appearance, behavior, some of which can be "proven" and some of which is at the stage of theory, to be verified as time goes on. Religion speaks not of the process itself nor the facts about observable objects and phenomena and their relationships, but about how to interpret the world that science so brilliantly describes for us; what view to take of it; what it all means to us in our lives.

With the eyes of faith we see this entire created order as revealing God's purpose. We believe that God's creative and sustaining power lie back of the natural world in all its variety and vastness. We believe also that human beings live in the universe because of God's creative work. Each of us, as well as all our ancestors, owes his life to God, who is continually active in creation. When a man and a woman through sexual union bring into life a human being, they are cooperating in a biological process which God purposed in the beginning. When the man and woman love and care for each other, their act of creation is in a small way kin to God's action in creation; they are fulfilling God's plan. Thus, human beings take their place in God's whole created world as responsible persons.

The faith that everything and everybody come from God is phrased with clarity and beauty by John, the evangelist:

22

In the beginning was the Word, and the Word
was with God, and the Word was God. He was
in the beginning with God; all things were made
through him, and without him was not anything
made that was made. In him was life, and the
life was the light of men. The light shines in the
darkness, and the darkness has not overcome it.

—JOHN 1:1–5

LIVING IN GOD'S WORLD

When we believe that we are persons created by the
purpose of God, born into God's world, what does this
mean for us today?

One of the most important meanings is that the created
order—the physical setting of human life—is cosmos and
not chaos. Cosmos refers to a universe which is orderly and
reliable, which can be described and explained in reasonable terms. Chaos is the condition of disorder in which
things happen for no explainable reason, in which nothing
is dependable and things are mixed up in hopeless confu-
sion. Life as we know it would be impossible in chaos.
Sometimes we get a small and brief experience of this
condition when some areas of existence become chaotic.
Chaos is likely to result in times of war or in some natural
upheaval such as a severe earthquake. In this situation
people find that their formerly accepted ways of doing
things are disrupted, and that the things they have always
counted on, such as the normal processes of law and order
or material resources, have been destroyed or changed.

So it is obvious that we could not live for long if such a condition were characteristic of our whole universe. When we read in the newspapers of the situation following an earthquake, often the reports say the first assistance rendered from the outside was to "restore order." Only then can medical and other aid be supplied, the debris cleared away, utilities restored, rebuilding started, and planning for the future undertaken. Because we do live in what is usually experienced as a cosmos, scientists have been able to learn about earthquakes from the history of the behavior of the earth's crust. They can help us understand why and how they happen, and deal more efficiently with the possibility of quakes. They cannot prevent or control earthquakes, at least not now. But already they have shown us how to predict weather, how to control floods.

It is good to remind ourselves that men have not always been able to understand the natural order in this way. Many long generations of human history were required before people learned the scientific explanation of such a happening as an earthquake. Before then most people responded to events in the natural world with magic. Because they had no way to probe beneath these events for the cause, they tried to ward off the dangers by appealing to gods who they believed resided in natural objects. Today we can state the causes of earthquakes in scientific terms, and so our fear is not based upon superstition and ignorance but upon an accurate reading of the probable danger involved. Knowing some ways to guard against the danger, our fears are more reasonable, and have less power over us.

The mistake we sometimes make today is that, having overcome superstition with scientific knowledge, we think that is the total picture. We do not go on to discover God's true relationship to the physical world and to ourselves as well. What is God saying to us through his creation? What does it mean to live in God's world?

In spite of occasional catastrophies like hurricanes which we do not yet know how to control, our physical environment is generally so dependable that we tend to take it for granted. Perhaps we do not recognize fully enough that as human beings we are able to organize our lives into orderly societies (with governments, schools, homes, business, cities, farms, churches) only because God has placed us in a universe which itself is orderly, a cosmos.

THE CHANGING WORLD

We said above that the order of God's world is not static and mechanical but dynamic. This means that change and development are as much a part of reality as stability and order. We see kinds of change all about us in the way a tree grows, the way a seed sprouts, the way a new strain of corn is developed, the way a baby learns to talk, the way a dog learns to respond to what you say to him, the way you become a more mature person. All these changes point to the fact that we live in a changing world because that is the way God planned it and us.

Some kinds of desirable change require a temporary disorder—that is, some breaking up of old patterns in order to build new ones. The seed destroys the seed case in which it has been enclosed so that it can sprout, put down a root, and grow into the bean or the petunia. Your dog suppresses his natural tendency to jump all over you in order to obey your command, "Down." Persons break out of old patterns of doing things—destroy old ways of behaving—in order to achieve better or more appropriate behavior. For example, they overcome "natural" self-centered behavior in order to become cooperative in their relationships with others. We should not put such a high value on any present kind of order that we cannot see the necessity of breaking into that order to bring about desirable change. Personal and family habits, the way our school does things, the set policies of our clubs or our communities or churches or nation are all subject to change as better ways are found.

YOU LIVE IN A GOOD WORLD

". . . and God saw that it was good." This is the way the Bible says God thought about his created universe. The Bible also suggests that God expects us to recognize, to use, and to enjoy the rich resources of the natural world. So what does it mean to say the universe is "good"?

When we realize this purpose of God, we can be sure that no part of his creation is unclean. No natural process or object is in itself foul. This understanding does away with many fears that have worried people in the past and that worry some people today. For example, people used to think that the disease of leprosy was "unclean" and that lepers should be feared and shunned. Today some persons take this same attitude toward cancer. Because cancer is not now fully understood and controllable, it seems mysterious and thus gives rise to unreasonable fears. Similarly, some people are frightened by serious mental retardation or shrink from the sight of a physical abnormality.

Such attitudes are out of harmony with the real character of natural processes. Disease and physical and mental abnormalities are not "unclean"; they are unfortunate, and sometimes tragic, circumstances of human life. Often they can be explained, guarded against, and prevented or cured by scientific means. Persons who are ill—even when the illness has something offensive about it like the odor that accompanies some forms of cancer, or something frightening, like unpredictable behavior—are not the victims of some evil power or unclean circumstance. They are our fellow human beings, victims of natural circumstances some of which are not yet understood, and others we are gradually learning to control.

The same principle is true of the ordinary and daily processes of human hygiene; there is nothing "dirty" about them although we consider some of them private, which is different. Rather they are a part of God's creation to be understood and dealt with in the interest of our physical health.

Natural catastrophe (for example, the earthquake spoken of above) is not "evil" in the sense that God is using this means to punish people. People suffer in such disasters, but they suffer as a result of a natural event not yet fully understood by men. Sometimes, however, persons suffer in such a natural disaster because they did not take the necessary precautions. For example, in the Alaska earthquake of 1964 those buildings were not destroyed which had been constructed according to facts men had learned about how a structure may withstand a possible earthquake. Most floods of recent years, the engineers tell us, could have been avoided if men had used the knowledge already available to them about the conservation and control and storage of water.

To say the universe is "good" does not mean that people will never run into any trouble with it or that it is now fully understood. Rather it means that, in the main, the universe yields to investigation, and that it will support man in health and happiness if properly approached and used.

All of us have experiences of happiness in God's world —in fact, for most persons these happy experiences are much more numerous than the unhappy ones. Call to mind the beauties of creation: the graceful curves of a seagull in flight; the peaks of the Rockies thrust against the sky in harsh, gray angles; the black, boiling clouds and sharp streaks of lightning in a thunderstorm; the vibrant yellows and scarlets of the hard maple tree in October; a geranium unfolding its red petals in a window box.

Call to mind also the joy of participation in God's

natural world: the cool, swift flow of water past your face and shoulders as your precise flutter kick carries you from one end of the pool to the other; a tumble in the snow or a walk in the rain; the feel of rough sand or bouncy blades of grass against your bare feet; the fun of using your body in skillful ways in football, or skiing, or skating. Remember, too, the exhilarating sense of discovery as you solve a mathematical equation, or see the pattern in a spectroscope identifying an element in the stars, or the intricate structures of invisible life-forms viewed through a microscope.

The natural setting of our lives provides almost endless opportunity for joy and participation and discovery. Also, as was said above, nature sustains our lives through its resources of minerals, fibers, foods, fuels, building materials. Life is sustained in another way—by the delicate balance between animal and plant life, and by the atmosphere surrounding our planet which shields us from the killing heat and the killing cold of space, and thus establishes a livable climate for human beings.

In all these and many other ways the created world is "good." God's purpose is that we shall enjoy it, explore it, understand it, and take responsibility for using it for the sustaining of life and for the health and happiness of all persons.

RESPECTING GOD'S CREATION

All along we have referred to the universe as "God's world," his creation. What this phrase says to us is that this is not "our world." We live in it, and God has given us some responsibility for it and some control over it. But the world and all created life still belong to God. This means that nature, in its many expressions from stars to coal mines, from wheat fields to beehives, possesses a sacred or moral quality. That is, the physical universe has value in itself, is worthy of man's respect as well as available for his use. Here is an illustration of what this means in our everyday lives. The leader of a craft group is talking to some young people.

"This is a piece of walnut. See its glowing brown color and the way the grain in the wood makes an interesting fluid pattern. This short length of lumber was once part of a tall, healthy tree in some forest. It took a long time and a complex process of growth to produce this tree from a walnut seed in its hard shell. The tree, including this small part of it, grew according to God's natural laws—the same laws that may be observed in all of nature. Therefore we respect this piece of walnut as part of God's creation.

"All good craftsmen respect the materials with which they work. As good craftsmen we are not free to waste this wood, throw it on a dump, or mar it in any way. Instead, we intend to make of this wood something beautiful and useful which will give pleasure to many people. The person who works with it will use his best skill, not being careless or lazy in applying his tools, so that the value of this bit of God's world will be increased."

This attitude of having respect for and acting responsibly toward the natural world, of which we are a part, is our way of acknowledging its value, or sacred quality. Such an attitude is appropriate to the astronaut orbiting the earth, businessmen dealing in lumber or oil, the farmer tilling his field, members of Congress deciding what use will be made of certain seashore areas, the Boy Scout lighting a camp fire, the nuclear physicist working on mathematical formulas. These people, indeed all of us, are not free in God's sight to do anything they want to do with the world of nature, to use it for any purpose they may decide on, or to destroy it irresponsibly. For human beings to use the created world in such ways that the soil is eroded and made unproductive, that streams or lakes are polluted so they cannot sustain fish and provide essential water for men and animals, that air is poisoned so it is dangerous to breathe—such use is deliberately to undermine the value of the created world, and to go against the purpose of God for the world.

Rather, men are to use nature in harmony with God's purpose for his created world; that is, to sustain life and to bring joy and benefit to all people. In so doing they are affirming the sacred or moral quality of creation. They are acknowledging that it came from God and belongs to God; that man is both dependent upon it and responsible for taking care of it.

So when persons ask, "Where did I come from?" the answer of faith is that we come from God as part of his whole created world. This answer was affirmed long ago in the Bible and it is also verified in the experience of men today.

However, there is something more. Although persons are part of creation, they are not altogether like the rest of creation. There are important differences between persons and other forms of life. This thought brings us straight to the second question, "Who Am I?"

2.

WHO AM I?

WHEN you wonder about the kind of person you are; when you want to know what makes you act the way you do; when you question whether you are able to be or to achieve something you want to be or to do— you are asking one of life's basic questions: Who am I? You may not phrase the question in this way, and you may not even be conscious of it as a question. But all wonderment about what you are like, what you can do, how you may behave in specific situations, is an effort to understand yourself.

Self-understanding is important for you, and for every person. With more or less accurate knowledge of yourself you can direct your life with more intelligence, and make plans both for the present and the future with more confidence. To understand yourself is to take one of the giant steps toward becoming the person you want to be. The beginning of self-understanding comes quite early in life, but ability to deal with this question directly and consciously develops in a special way in the teen years. This is the time when you first really come to grips with who you are.

I AM A PART OF GOD'S CREATED WORLD

As we said in the first chapter, you are here in this world because of God's purpose in creation, which accounts for the universe and all life within it, and also for human beings, as a part of that life. The first thing to be said then about who you are is that you are a part of creation. Your physical body is a part of the total physical world, sharing the same physical elements—carbon, phosphorous, oxygen, and the like—and subject to the same physical laws. A human being is as subject to the law of gravity, for example, as the planet Venus in its orbit around the sun. Technologists must make very special arrangements to use laws in new ways when an astronaut "walks in space" outside the pull of gravity from the earth. As the world of nature follows laws, persons also in the physical side of their lives follow the same laws. All creation makes sense in this way.

You can quickly see how significant this fact is for us. We do not live in an environment that is strange and uncongenial to us. On the contrary, as we saw in the previous chapter, our physical environment is so much a part of what we are that it sustains our lives and provides pleasure and enjoyment. Also, man's relationship to the natural order means that the physical processes of the human body, operating according to God's natural laws, can be understood and controlled and even predicted to a high degree. This understanding makes possible the practice of medicine. It makes possible athletic skills, beautiful and rhythmic movements in the ballet, and the sheer fun and joy of climbing hills, playing games, swimming, skating, dancing. And because the body can be controlled and trained, man can create pictures and play musical instruments and use his strength and skill to do all sorts of useful work. Thus your physical body is important.

There is, however, a second and more important fact about who you are. Although human beings are in many ways like the rest of creation, they have some distinctive characteristics that make them different from the rest of the natural world. So far as we know now, only human beings have the capacity of self-consciousness; that is, of being able to see and observe and think about themselves as part of God's world. This is what you are doing as you read this book—thinking about yourself. Human beings also have the unique ability to stand apart from the natural world, to explore and describe it. Modern science, one of man's highest achievements, has developed from this special capacity of man. Human beings are different from the other animals also in having some specialized physical equipment, for example, the highly developed human brain.

I AM DIFFERENT

The Bible helps us to affirm this truth about who we are. The first chapter of Genesis says, "Then God said, 'Let us make man in our image, after our likeness; and let them have dominion over the fish of the sea, and over the birds of the air, and over the cattle, and over all the earth, and over every creeping thing that creeps upon the earth.' So God created man in his own image, in the image of God he created him." In the second chapter we read, "Then the Lord God formed man of dust from the ground, and breathed into his nostrils the breath of life; and man became a living being."

These two verses come from two ancient accounts of the creation. The one in the second chapter is probably earlier in origin than the one in the first chapter. When we put together these two biblical interpretations of God's creative action, we can understand them to mean that although human beings are made from the "dust of the earth" (that is, of the same stuff as the rest of creation), men are also made "in the image of God," "after his likeness." In other words, as human beings we are different because we have God's mark upon us; there is something in us or about us that is like God himself.

The ancient Hebrews who viewed the creation of human beings in this way had discovered a great religious truth. They were not describing in scientific terms the long development of man; but under the inspiration of God they were describing who man is, and his unique place in all of creation. This is a statement of religious faith. The biblical writers did not understand the many ways God takes to bring forth his creation; and the wisest scientist today does not fully understand them. Perhaps men never will. God and his ways are so far beyond our human capacity fully to understand that we can never know God completely.

It seems clear, however, that God does not wish to remain hidden from man. He reveals himself to us in many ways and supports our efforts to know him, our response to his revelations. In fact, we believe that the urge, as well as the capacity, to explore and discover the truth about God and his world is a special gift to man from God. It is man's nature to want to explore and discover.

I AM CREATED IN GOD'S IMAGE

To be created "in God's image" has very important meanings for all human beings. Let us consider them briefly.

The word "image" means "a reflection of." The reflection of yourself in a mirror is an image of yourself; so is your picture on a photographic print. People say of a child that "he's the image of his father," meaning that the child looks and perhaps acts like his father. The child is not his father, and your mirrored image or your photograph is not you. But there is much of you in your reflection or photograph; people can get some idea of what you are like from these images. This is what the long-ago accounts of creation are saying about God and human beings. They are like God in some respects because they are created in his image. Thus we say human beings are "persons," and persons are unique in God's creation.

I AM A PERSON

Because you are a person you possess certain distinctive capacities and capabilities. The most important of these is that you can respond to God, can know he cares about you as a person. This is because you are created in the image of God. You also have other distinctive capacities.

For instance, you have learned intellectual skills such as reading and writing. Along with these basic language skills, you have the capacity to analyze and organize. When you watch a ball game and later tell someone who did not see it why your side made more home runs than the other side, you are analyzing the ball game. You are not only describing what happened but you are also figuring out why it happened. You use your powers of analysis in many ways. Suppose your father's car won't start. You suggest that perhaps there is no gasoline in the tank, or the fuel line is stopped up, or the battery is weak, and you begin to investigate these possibilities. In the same way you analyze other problems, such as those in an arithmetic lesson or those that come up when you are learning to use a new camera; or a new dress pattern; or those harder ones that come up in getting along with other people. Analyzing a problem is the first step in solving it.

Another unique capacity of human beings is shown in

our use of tools and machines. The invention of the wheel in ancient times and of the electronic computer in modern times grew out of this capacity which enables men to design and to make and use tools to serve their needs and purposes.

Because you are a person you have also the power of imagination. Through your thoughts and feelings you can dream up something new: new ways of doing things or new ways of looking at things, new meanings in old things, or new connections among familiar things. Notice that the word "imagination" has the same root as the word "image." The imagination gets hold of and develops new or revised "images." This truly wonderful power has enabled persons throughout the ages to build civilizations through the arts, such as painting, sculpture; through the humanities, such as literature, language, law; through the sciences, such as biology, physics, sociology; through technology, such as buildings, dams, irrigation systems. You use your imagination when you write a theme or a story for an English class, when you rearrange the furniture in your room more attractively, when you devise a new play for your football team, when you see some new meaning in a verse from the Bible, or in a formula in mathematics, or in a drama or a symphony.

Added to these skills and powers are the twin abilities to plan and predict. You can plan and organize a picnic, predicting how long it will take to get to the picnic site and how much food you will need and whether or not the weather is likely to be favorable. At the beginning of a school year you can plan the courses you will take and organize a weekly schedule, predicting how much study time each will require, what each will contribute to your life both now and in the future.

I LIVE UNDER GOD'S MORAL LAW

The fact that you are a person has significance beyond even these powers, skills, and capacities. Your personhood also has moral significance. This means that persons, unique among God's creatures, have the capacity to distinguish between good and evil, and therefore to use their skills and powers for either good or evil purposes. For example, a person may use his imagination to find new ways of helping mankind, or to find new ways of destroying mankind; to make life happier for others, or to promote only his own advantage.

The story of Adam and Eve in the Garden of Eden tells us of the way in which these two persons, who were prototypes of all mankind, discovered the powers of both good and evil in themselves. This basic truth about persons—their capacity for good as God's creatures, and their human tendency to do evil—is confirmed in history. It is confirmed in our own experience. You know persons who are sometimes good and sometimes bad. You have seen your friends use their cleverness or popularity or power over people to support something good; at another time you have seen them use their influence for something not good. When you are honest you recognize the same thing in yourself. You know, when you take a frank and sober look, that you often do things that are bad, and also that often you are on the side of the good.

Why is it that persons—made in the image of God—are not always good? Is God that way, too? Or did he make us that way? Is he responsible for our evil tendencies? These first chapters in Genesis help us to answer these questions.

> So God created man in his own image, in the image of God he created him; male and female he created them. And God blessed them, and God said to them, 'Be fruitful and multiply, and fill the earth and subdue it; and have dominion over the fish of the sea and over the birds of the air and over every living thing that moves upon the earth.' And God said, 'Behold, I have given you every plant yielding seed which is upon the face of all the earth, and every tree with seed in its fruit; you shall have them for food. And to every beast of the earth, and to every bird of the air, and to everything that creeps on the earth, everything that has the breath of life, I have given every green plant for food.' And it was so. And God saw everything that he had made, and behold, it was very good.
>
> —Genesis 1:27–31

Here we are assured that God's creation, including mankind, is good. (We saw part of what this means in Chapter One.) We are also told that God has given people power, responsibility, and freedom. Man is to have "dominion over every living thing." This fact gives us the clue in dealing with our questions. God intends good through his creation, especially man created in God's image. At the same time, God endows persons with freedom to make their own choices. They are free to make choices between good and evil; they are free to use their powers of "dominion" in good ways or in evil ways. If this were not so, men would not be persons but puppets or robots. So part of being a person is to possess the power to make choices.

I AM FREE AND RESPONSIBLE

When we read on in Chapters 2 and 3 of Genesis, we find that Adam and Eve did indeed exercise their freedom. They denied God and chose to do evil. This is what is called sin: to disobey God; to choose one's own way instead of God's way; to choose evil instead of good. And we see in the story that Adam and Eve suffered the consequences of this choice.

Thus the Bible tells us that persons are not only free; they are also responsible. They are responsible to God who created them in his image, to be his children. God's purpose for his children is good. But God does not *make* us respond to his good purposes. This means that while we as human beings may make our own decisions in life, we are responsible for those decisions. We must take the consequences of our decisions, good or bad.

And how exciting it is, that this is so! To be both free and responsible means that we have the power to make choices, and that our choices make sense because we can observe or even experience their outcomes or consequences. You can see evidence of such outcomes every day. This truth revealed in the Bible and experienced by us in daily life is that moral law is as sure and dependable as physical law. When we go against moral law, we bring upon ourselves the consequences of this disobedience. To love and trust God means that we seek to live in accordance with his moral law, and so to enjoy the satisfactions of feeling "at home" with God, in companionship with him as our Father.

God's moral law gives us a lot of assurance, and even confidence. It assures us that we are not at the mercy of the evil in the world or the tendency to sin in ourselves. God has acted in the world for good. He acted in creation. He acted in history. He acted in Jesus Christ. God also is acting now. He calls men to act, too. In response to God, we can do something about evil. We can count on God's care and guidance as we make the choices that make up our lives.

Thus, an answer to our question is that the freedom we have as persons makes possible the evil in the world and in ourselves, but we are not bound by this evil although we may suffer on account of it. With God's help, we may overcome evil with good. God's care for us never slackens even when we are disobedient. His steadfast, seeking love does not cease even when we do not respond to it.

I AM NOT PERFECT

We must go a little further, however, if we are to understand ourselves. The next idea to get hold of is very important. Although persons are made in the image of God and reflect some of the characteristics of God, human beings are not God. God is infinite, unconditioned, unchanging. As the Psalmist said, "From everlasting to everlasting thou art God." Human beings, on the other hand, are conditioned, limited, dependent, and finite.

What do these words mean in our practical lives? For one thing, they mean that each human being is himself and nobody else. He is given certain conditions or characteristics at birth through the natural process of heredity, and nothing he can do will change these basic conditions. For example, your sex is determined, your race is determined, and you are given certain physical characteristics such as body type and shape of the skeleton, color and shape of eyes. Also certain developments of your physical and psychological makeup are predictable at birth. There may be a weakness of some organ, possibly the lungs, or a special strength, possibly a very good heart. The tension of your nervous system may be high or low, which will have something to do with whether you are generally a high-strung or a relaxed person. You may have a special capacity for singing or for figuring out mathematical formulas. Usually each individual receives some things at birth which later he recognizes as advantages, and other things he regards as disadvantages.

44

One of the learnings you can master while you are a young person is to assess your "conditions"—the things about yourself that you must live with. If you are honest and realistic, you will find that some of them are assets and others are liabilities. When you have looked squarely at your assets and capacities, you will do whatever you can to develop them as fully as you can. When you have looked squarely at those liabilities which you cannot change, you will do whatever you can to adjust to them without bitterness or self-pity. Learning to be grateful for your assets, and to accept your liabilities without wasting effort in feeling sorry about them is an important step forward. To grow up in this way will add to your personal comfort and happiness all your life.

I MUST ACCEPT MYSELF

To be limited and finite means that you can't do everything, be everywhere, possess unlimited power, nor attain perfection. This fact of life seems so obvious that no one would ever question it. But people do question it, especially people who do not understand and accept themselves because they do not know who they are. You may know people who want to be able to do everything everyone else does, or people who are disappointed with themselves when they do not measure up to some overly high expectations, or who wail over the fact that they can't be in two places at the same time—even in such simple cases as the conflicting Thanksgiving dinner at Grandma's and the football game at school. All our lives we are subject to such limitations as these because we are finite human beings.

It is up to each of us, then, to come to terms with our human limitations. This means having reasonable expectations for ourselves, and for other people, making smart choices among alternatives, saying "no" to some and "yes" to others because it is not possible to be or to do everything. It means recognizing that nothing in life is perfect except God, and so being willing and able to accept imperfection without too much disappointment—the dance where you had something less than a good time, the game you didn't win, the friend who has let you down, the job you didn't land.

There is a deeper dimension, too. Being human also means that we shall not always succeed even when what we seek to do is something good. We shall sometimes fail to be a friend in need or to do as well as we could in school. We shall sometimes fail to do what we know we should do, to stand for what we know is right. At such times we feel like saying with Paul, "The good that I would do, I do not, and the evil that I would not, that I do!"

Does all this sound like a grim prospect? Well, it really is not. Once you become realistic about your limitations and your assets, you have added to your self-understanding. From this base you can use all your gifts and capacities in realistic rather than wishful ways. Thus you can live a full and satisfying life, knowing that no human being can be or do or have everything he longs for. This is why we could say two paragraphs back that growing up in self-understanding, far from being grim, gives the kind of security from which comfort and happiness may come.

I LIVE AMONG OTHER PEOPLE

To begin to find out about yourself, to grow in self-understanding, brings up questions about other people. This is so because apparently a person is not a full self except as he comes into relationship with other selves. Indeed, we find out much about ourselves from other people; the way they think about us influences to some extent the way we think about ourselves. Evidently persons are created to be together; we are social by nature. All of us are aware that literally we spend our lives with other people. Few of us could be happy all alone.

And so we come to the question: Who are these other people? The quick reply is they are persons, too; just as you are a person. This reply, however, is too quick and easy unless we dig below the surface to discover what the statement really means. The meaning, here, is very interesting, possibly unexpected, and even disturbing.

To begin with, all humankind, all persons everywhere and of all times, are equally dependent upon the Creator God. Further, it is God's purpose that all persons be children of God. Though each one is unique in his personhood, they are also much alike—you and me and all of us. Psychologists tell us that people are alike at least in these ways: Their physical bodies are alike in general makeup and the way the various physical systems function—blood, nerves, muscles, lungs; emotionally, they are alike in their basic needs—to survive, to have security and affection, to achieve; they are alike in their special powers—to choose and plan as persons; and they are alike in their capacity for and tendencies toward both good and evil.

But it is obvious as we look around us that persons also are different from one another. They differ in looks, in the way they behave, in what they want, in what they achieve, and in many other ways. We have seen how some people have some assets and liabilities and other people have different ones. Here we must make a distinction between *who* a person is and *what* or how he is.

I LIVE WITHIN DIVERSITY

Every person is of equal importance with every other person in the sight of God. The differences we observe among persons arise primarily because of who their ancestors were, where they live, what has happened to them and to their forefathers in the past, the kind of society of which they are a part.

The fact that all persons are of the same order of creation and are basically alike does not mean that they are all equal in their individual capacities. Some are smart and some are stupid, some are artistic and some insensitive to beauty, some energetic and some lazy. These differences are usually accounted for by circumstances of heredity, birth, and environment.

Again, individuals are not alike in the way they develop their capacities. Some slow learners accomplish more than some smart persons; some physically handicapped persons do more than some physically strong persons. Also, persons are not alike in the way they deal with their innate tendencies to good and evil. Some persons triumph over the evil in themselves more than others do; but no one of us triumphs all the time. Some persons are more concerned about and do more to overcome the evils in society than do others; and no one of us knows all about how to cure all these evils.

Many differences we observe in persons are due to climate, diet, and other aspects of their physical environment, as well as the particular culture they live in. For instance, southern Europeans differ from northern Europeans, generally, in body type, hair color and texture, and skin tone. The persons from northern Germany probably will look different from the persons from southern Italy. In the United States these physical characteristics are all mixed up because both northern Europeans and southern Europeans—and many others—have been a part of the United States for several generations.

Culture means the sum of the ways a group of people have organized to live together. It includes the customs and social arrangements and the religious faith they live by and the values they cherish. As an example of differences in social customs among peoples, in the United States and most western societies it is the custom to shake hands when meeting people, whereas in Japan it is the custom to make a formal bow. The meaning of the act is the same; but the way the meaning is expressed is different. (On the other hand, a smile is an act of communication which has a place and a similar meaning in many cultures.) In most western societies men wear trousers; but in many eastern societies they wear skirts of various kinds. This difference was originally due to such matters as climate and occupation, and availability of materials. Sheep for wool have been historically common in Europe; whereas the silkworm and silk culture have historically been common in Asia.

As situations change and people from diverse societies learn from one another, customs change, too. We see this happening today at a very rapid rate. In Tokyo, for example, most businessmen now wear western suits during the day; while quite recently I read in a fashion magazine that men in the United States are finding the loose robe, worn by Japanese men at home, very satisfactory as a leisure indoor garment. World travel is demonstrating that the differences between a businessman in Singapore and one in Muncie, Indiana; or a schoolboy in Moscow and one in Washington; or a mother in Liberia and one in Norway are superficial and external, while basic human similarities are universal.

One of the big factors in making for differences among people is opportunity. Societies develop according to the opportunities that come to them. For example, the United States and other western societies have developed a high order of technology. At a simple level this means that in western societies men have turned their intelligence toward the invention of machines of various kinds. In eastern societies, until recent times, men have turned their intelligence primarily toward the arts and philosophy, rather than the products of industry. The historical opportunities in Europe and Asia were different.

Sometimes a society remains static or unchanging because it is cut off by geography from other societies, and so it persists in an "undeveloped" stage, as we say today. In other words, opportunity for development has not been present. This was true in the past of some societies in the interior of Africa.

I RESPOND TO DIVERSITY

When we reflect upon the diversity of humankind, yet our unity as human beings created in God's image, we can't help but appreciate the richness of human life. The fact that we don't all speak the same language, nor look alike, nor do things the same way, nor enjoy the same music or art, nor think alike, nor want the same things makes our lives together on this planet exciting and stimulating.

But this diversity can also make us fearful. It seems that most persons are afraid of the unfamiliar. Strange talk or strange ways sometimes make us nervous and uncomfortable. And we express this fear in different ways, depending upon how strong it is. Sometimes the fear of the strange and the different is so strong that we want to do away with these other people. We excuse ourselves, unconsciously perhaps, by saying that their ways are "bad" and exert a "bad influence" on "our people." Yet by "bad" we may mean only "different from us." Or we may express this fear in ridicule, saying how absurd or how quaint these "other people" are. Or we may ignore these strange and different people, excluding them and drawing away from them into our own group where the ways are familiar and not upsetting.

Actually, though, such fear of differences is not warranted. Only in rare circumstances do we face any danger just because something is strange or different. Two thoughts might help us keep in check such fear. They are: The people we consider "strange" or "different" are thinking the same thing about us! They are afraid, too. Do they have anything to fear from us? And the second thought is: All—"we" and "they"—are part of God's creation, having the same basic characteristics and the same basic human needs.

We might add a third thought: Why not learn from our interesting differences and enjoy God's good world together?

Let us return to those questions people ask about themselves with which we started this chapter. Only the individual himself can find the particular answers that apply to him. But we have put forward some general points of view that may help that one person—maybe you. We have seen that every human being is created by God in his image, with the potential powers, capacities, and limitations of personhood, yet each one is unique; that each person is free and responsible, yet each one is subject to God's moral law. It helps the whole human family for each member to understand not only himself but also his neighbors, to know that everyone is alike in many ways; and to recognize at the same time the many interesting individual and cultural differences among people which give color and excitement to our life together.

The basic truth is that we are all children of God and called by God to be who we are: each one his own unique self, yet each one a part of the human family.

3.

WHAT AM I
HERE FOR?

CHUCK was sitting on the back steps eating an apple and watching his baby brother in a playpen. Chuck was scowling, and once in a while between bites of the apple his mouth would get tight. Then he threw the apple core over the baby's head and gave a big, deep sigh.

Chuck was asking himself some questions, and the scowl probably meant that he wasn't getting any satisfactory answers.

"Why do I have to do this?" he was saying to himself. "It isn't my job to mind this baby. I don't have anything to do with him; I could be over at Ted's working on our model airplane. Why do I have to do this? Why can't I do what I want to?" His scowl turned into a thoughtful frown. "What is life all about?" he wondered. "What am I here for anyway?"

Almost everyone has been in situations like Chuck's many times—situations that raise one of those basic questions in life: What am I here for? Or stated another way: What is the purpose of life; what am I supposed to be doing with it? Chuck was asking very natural, and in fact, necessary questions about his life. Was he supposed to be a baby sitter? Wasn't there something better than that for him in life?

Sitting there looking at the baby and resenting his chore, Chuck was taking a short view. He would recognize this if he gave it a little thought. Of course, his whole life was not baby sitting! But very often it's the short view, the immediate, unsatisfactory situations that cause people to feel resentful. In order to handle such situations and not to be thrown by them, we must bring them out into the open and discover some ways of dealing with them.

No one of us asked to be born. We did not choose the time nor place of our birth; and we could not select our parents. Even so, here we are with our own abilities and limitations, our own families and nation and race and culture, with the world all about us, and near the beginning of our personal lives. So we wonder: Why, and to what end or purpose, am I here?

To struggle for some answers to these questions that make sense of our lives is better than drifting unaware from day to day and letting the short view dominate our horizon. A recognized and accepted overall view of life helps us to see some meaning in all its events, big and little. This purpose also helps us to direct events. Some things seem just to happen to us; other things we can make happen or keep from happening. No one is ever in complete control of his life; but no one has to be completely without control of his life.

MAN'S COVENANT WITH GOD

We said earlier that there were some sources to which we look for help in finding answers to our important questions, and that an important source in finding answers is religious faith. The Bible contains the record of the faith of many generations. Let's see what it tells us about why we are here.

Reading along in the book of Genesis after the story of creation, we find Adam and Eve, who represent all human beings, establishing a household, having children, and generally taking up life in the world; that is, outside the Garden of Eden. Their grandchildren and many times great-grandchildren continue the story. All the rest of the Bible has to do with God's effort to reveal to these ancient people what life is all about, and with their effort to understand and live by what God is saying and doing. Sometimes they succeeded and sometimes they failed, just as we do today.

A key event in this long story is recounted in the story of the Flood. In this ancient and strange story is pictured one of the greatest leaps of faith that any .people has ever made. Scholars tell us that very likely the race memory of a wide-spread flood in the distant past is the basis of this biblical account. The Hebrew writers of a later day, inspired by God's spirit, used this story of Noah and his family who survived the flood in an ark not so much to recount ancient history as to interpret its meaning for their own religious faith.

This meaning is caught up in a symbol—the rainbow. After the flood waters had subsided and the ground was dry, Noah and his family left the ark. Before doing anything else, Noah made a point of thanking God for being saved from the flood. We read:

> Then Noah built an altar to the Lord, and took of every clean animal and of every clean bird, and offered burnt offerings on the altar. And when the Lord smelled the pleasing odor, the Lord said in his heart, "I will never again curse the ground because of man, for the imagination of man's heart is evil from his youth; neither will I ever again destroy every living creature as I have done. While the earth remains, seedtime and harvest, cold and heat, summer and winter, day and night, shall not cease."
>
> Then God said to Noah and to his sons with him, "Behold, I establish my covenant with you and your descendants after you."
>
> And God said, "This is the sign of the covenant which I make between me and you and every living creature that is with you, for all future generations: I set my bow in the cloud and it shall be a sign of the covenant between me and the earth."
>
> —GEN. 8:20–22; 9:8–9, 12–13.

The great leap of faith is the covenant symbolized by the rainbow. A covenant is a promise which is willingly made and binding on both sides. What this covenant meant was that these early Hebrews believed that their God was powerful and loyal and responsible; that his word to his people could be depended on and that he would care for his people, who in turn would be faithful to him in worship and in following his purposes. The remarkable thing about this faith of the early Hebrews is that no other people of their time whom we know about possessed this kind of understanding of and faith in God. Other peoples believed their gods were irresponsible, vengeful, and unconcerned about people. So the ancient Hebrews, led by Noah, made a covenant with their God of which the rainbow was a sign.

The remainder of the Old Testament tells in many ways how God kept his side of the promise; how he dealt with his people, how he loved and disciplined them, how he rescued them in trouble, and raised up leaders to guide them according to his purposes. We see God acting in this way in the stories of Abraham, Jacob, and Joseph; in the experiences of Moses, David, and the prophets. The people of Israel through the long generations learned more and more of what life is all about, what its purpose is, what it means to be a child of God individually, and together to be the people of God. The Hebrews, (later called the Children of Israel) just as people today, were sometimes faithful to the covenant they had made with God, and sometimes unfaithful and disobedient. They learned that life involves problems and opportunities, danger and security, challenges and joys, failures and triumphs. They learned through it all that God is dependable, and that God expects his people to be responsible.

GOD'S PURPOSE FOR HIS CHILDREN

In this long history of the Hebrew people as recounted in the Old Testament we recognize one of the great messages of the Bible for people today: Life is not an accident, it is not meaningless and arbitrary. Also, life is not absurd, although it may be comic and at times cruel. On the contrary, we learn from the Bible that the experiences of life may be understood because human existence, in which each personal life shares, has significance according to God's purpose. God's promise to his people is that if they will listen, he will make known that significance and guide them in trying to understand it. Thus they will be able to live life to the full.

In order for us to be aware of the meaning of life, however, we must fulfill our part of the covenant; we must keep man's side of the promise. That means we must be faithful and responsive to God, using our considerable powers as human beings to understand what God is saying to us. Then as understanding begins and grows we must respond, be obedient to his word. We are able thus to respond to God's purpose, because, as we saw in the previous chapter, we have been created in the image of God, capable of having fellowship with him. We are free and responsible persons who can understand, think, plan, and make choices.

To discover that life is meaningful is to go a long way in dealing with the question: What am I here for? Surely to believe that one is created as a person in the image of God and to share in human existence which has meaning and direction, is to recognize that I am here for some truly significant purpose. And so we come to a second great message of the Bible: The purpose of God for each person is that he shall participate fully in life, recognizing the meaning and significance of life's experiences and taking part freely and responsibly as a child of God. God intends that we shall *affirm* life: that we shall *choose* life and in a very real sense to "live it up."

LIVING ACCORDING TO GOD'S PURPOSE

There is no blueprint in the Bible showing how to participate in life as a child of God. No rules and regulations have been drawn that are appropriate for every time and place, for every individual person in every specific circumstance. Instead, the Bible, viewing us as free and responsible persons, called to live as children of God, reveals eternal values and fundamental principles by which we make everyday decisions and shape our lives. We have been endowed by God with powers of thought, analysis, and imagination which we are expected to use fully in making our own decisions in light of these fundamentals.

What are these basic principles and values? They are

summarized for men in the record of the life and teachings of Jesus Christ who lived among men. He showed men what God is like and what God's purposes for his children are. He told his followers that the purposes of God for his children may be summed up in two great commandments: "You shall love the Lord your God with all your heart, and with all your soul, and with all your mind. This is the great and first commandment. And a second is like it: You shall love your neighbor as yourself. On these two commandments hang all the law and the prophets." (Matt. 22:37-40).

To love God in this way means to put God first in life; in each situation we meet to ask first, "What sort of person does God plan for me to be? What does God want me to do in this situation?" And it means to want, more than anything else, to be and to do what God purposes. To love my neighbor as myself means to care about others, what happens to them, just as much as I care about myself and what happens to me. It means asking in any situation, "What is good for me?" and also asking at the same time and just as seriously, "What is good for my neighbor?" And it means, in deciding what to do, to be just as concerned about what it will mean to my neighbor's welfare, as about what it will mean to my own welfare. This way of loving my neighbor does not come easily. In fact, a human being cannot do it by himself. But, when a person does love God, and responds to his guidance, then a person can come to love his neighbor in this way.

In another saying, Jesus expressed the same idea in

these familiar words: "Whatever you wish that men would do to you, do so to them." And then he added to it something even harder: "Love your enemies and pray for those who persecute you so that you may be sons of your Father who is in heaven."

Again, in what have come to be called the Beatitudes, Jesus helped his disciples to know what makes a good life for men. His words give us today clues to answers to our important questions about life (MATT. 5:1-11). As we read these words in the English translation they may sound rather gloomy. But in the interpretation of Jesus' meaning they suggest clearly a way of laying hold on life that is good and that brings human happiness.

Those persons are really happy, Jesus says,
  *who know their own limitations and are eager to
    learn from God,*
  who truly care about others,
  *who are not proud and aggressive in asserting their
    own worth and importance,*
  who want and work for what is right and good,
  *who show mercy to those who wrong them,
    and compassion to those who suffer,*
  *who seek to think clearly about themselves and oth-
    ers and to act from pure motives,*
  *who recognize all men as brothers and so seek to live
    in peace and to bring others to live in peace,*
  *who stand firmly for what they believe is God's way
    in spite of what others say and even in spite of
    hardships and persecution.*

Jesus told men that these ways of living are the ways which bring men to true blessedness and fullness of life. And he ended the Beatitudes with the words, "Rejoice and be glad." Thus he affirmed that life in obedience to God's plan may not be easy, but it will not be gloomy or dull or meaningless; it will be joyous and exciting and satisfying.

Another important word of Jesus to his disciples says, "If you continue in my word, you are truly my disciples, and you shall know the truth and the truth will make you free." Thus, we learn that as we seek to do what we come to know is God's way for us, we shall learn more and more of the truth about ourselves and about our human relations and about our world. And as we learn more and more truth we shall be able increasingly to experience real freedom—freedom to think, to make decisions, to control ourselves, to act responsibly in the world.

Now let's take a brief look at what life is like for us today, and consider how we may make decisions about it in light of the principles and values we have found in these sayings.

ACCEPTING LIFE'S CHALLENGES TODAY

One way of describing life as we live it today is to say that it is made up of challenges and opportunities. The way any person responds to the challenges and opportunities of his experience makes up the quality of his personal life. As we have said earlier, those who have committed themselves to God in a covenant relationship will ask in each concrete situation: What kind of person would God have me be? What would God have me do at this time and in this place? The answers will issue in concrete decisions.

A survey of these aspects of life may help us to see what it means to participate in life as a child of God. What are some of these challenges?

1. THE CHALLENGE OF ADVENTURE

Life's challenges may be thought of as adventures. The life of any person may include big and little adventures. An adventure is any experience that involves a person in some exciting, unknown, and significant situation. This kind of situation produces surprises, calls forth a person's energies and imagination, reveals new meanings, opens up fresh avenues of discovery.

Adventures in life take many forms. One familiar form of adventure is the exploration of our planet, from the days of the early Phoenicians sailing their frail but seaworthy boats out into unknown waters, to the present-day explorations of the United States Navy in Antarctica. In this form of adventure a person leaves a familiar environment and pushes out into an unknown world to see what is there. Or one may go beyond this planet, become an astronaut and explore outer space, or perhaps even the moon.

New Situations

Although every person cannot explore some unknown sector of the universe like Antarctica, or outer space, nearly every young person today has the chance to explore some part of the world as yet unknown to him. When you move to a new neighborhood or a new town, when you change schools, when you travel to a part of your state or to another state where you have never been—or even go to a part of your city you have never seen—you are an explorer on an adventure. In a real sense you are entering an unknown world. This unfamiliar situation has the qualities of an adventure: surprise, discovery, and the calling forth of your energies and imagination. In these new worlds, you are likely to find something familiar that makes you feel at home. You are also likely to find many things that are unfamiliar, for example, a different climate, different ways of speech, or ways of doing things, differences in the personal habits of people, or the color of their skin. Such unfamiliar things may make you feel lonely, or uncomfortable, as if you don't belong. The feeling of not belonging can be very upsetting. But exactly here—at the point where you feel you don't belong—is the heart of the adventure. Here is where your energy and your imagination are required. Here is where the whole experience may become truly significant. Let's look at a few examples.

There is this new high school you are going to because your family has moved. You don't know your way around; you don't know any of the students or the teachers. You feel lost and a little frightened. You are homesick for your old gang, and there is a hard knot in your stomach. It would be quite natural for you to say, "What is adventurous about this?" One of the first rules in having an adventure turn out well is not to panic. So you try to relax. That will help the hard knot to disappear. You remember that a high school is a high school; that is to say, some things are much the same in most American high schools. Each has classrooms and a daily schedule, and extracurricular activities, and probably at least one person whose responsibility is to look after "new" students. With this help it should not be hard to figure out where you should be, and when, on any Monday morning.

You also remember that people are people. These particular persons may speak with an accent different from yours, and their behavior may be unusual from your standpoint, but in spite of that they are persons like you. They are likely to respond in many situations just as you would. So you use your imagination and say to yourself, "How would I have wanted a new student to act in my old school?" The first thing to occur to you may be that in your old school there was nothing the new student need be afraid of, so probably the same is true here. But, of course, you *are* new, and there's a lot you don't know. Recognizing what you don't know, and admitting it, is a mark of the true adventurer. Often this admission takes courage because it says to the world that you don't belong —yet. You have the potential of this kind of courage. What is required is that you put some energy behind this potential so that you freely admit you are new and don't know and start asking questions. You are, then, on the road to discovery: learning interesting things about the new high school community, adding to your life fresh experiences, making new friends.

It is quite probable that before the first term ends, you will feel as comfortable in this new high school as in an old shoe. We must take account of another possibility, however: that you may continue to feel strange, that you don't belong, in this high school. And there is the possibility that the new high school may *not* be as good a school as the old one was. As we said earlier, we do not live in a perfect world, and neither persons, including ourselves, nor institutions like schools are perfect. There are times when in spite of our best efforts things will not turn out favorably for us. Even so, you have ventured into unknown territory and have added to your store of knowledge and experience. You have learned to live with change. You can draw on this experience later in a time of need.

Meeting Difficult Conditions

Here is an adventure of a different kind. One sunny day during Christmas vacation in a southern state a troop of Boy Scouts arrived at a camp site where they were to spend a week. Three days later a heavy and unexpected snow fell in that territory. Life had handed these boys a challenge because none of them except the Scout Master had ever camped in tents in the snow. At first all they could think of was how cold and wet they were. Parents of the boys were thinking the same thing, and soon the highway patrol reached the camp and offered the Scouts transportation to their warm and comfortable homes. By that time, however, the boys had responded to this challenge by seeing it as an adventure. They used their ingenuity to figure out how they might keep warm and dry and fed in a snowy camp. And they used their energy in reorganizing their living arrangements according to a whole new plan. They thanked the patrolman but refused his offer of rescue because they were having the best camp ever. "The climbers on Everest," one boy quipped, "have nothing on us."

Going to a new school may be an adventure in relationships with people. Coping with snow at camp may be an adventure in living under difficult conditions without the usual comforts. A third type of adventure is the adventure of the mind, often the most rewarding of all.

Learning Something New

A high school sophomore was dismayed to find that two years of Latin were required for entrance into the college of her choice. "What can be more deadly than Latin?" she wailed, while debating whether to select another college. Here was one of life's challenges which she could ignore by going to another college, or which she could accept by putting her energies and her imagination to the task of finding out why Latin, of all things, was considered in some circles necessary to the educated person. It may seem odd to call starting the study of Latin an adventure. But that is how it turned out for this student. A whole new world opened up for her—a world of new information and understanding about the way in which the English language has been influenced by the Latin language. She discovered that many English-American institutions have their roots in Roman law and custom. "Even though we don't speak Latin on Main Street any more," she says now, "it certainly is not dead." Although Latin never became her favorite subject in school, she is appreciative of this adventure in learning.

Perhaps these examples illustrate the fact that life is full of things to do, to learn about, to accomplish, all of them having the possibility of making our lives richer and more satisfying. We will not recognize these possibilities, however, unless we put forth some effort. Every challenge that life offers makes demands on us—demands to take risks in entering the unknown, to mobilize our energies, to summon up our resources of stability, imagination, and ingenuity. If we are fearful of what is new or unfamiliar, if we are lazy or too much interested in being comfortable, we will let life's challenges and opportunities for adventure go by. We will settle deeper in a secure and cozy— and dull—rut. Our lives will be constricted; many of our powers as a person will remain untapped; and we will bypass many of the joys of human relationships.

2. Learning to Say "No"

One word of caution should be entered here. Sometimes life offers us a challenge that should be turned down firmly. Not all the opportunities for adventure will open up the good things of life. We must exercise judgment in any situation, a judgment that is based on an understanding of who we are—children of God—and of what is God's purpose for us.

Rusty thought it would be an exciting adventure to go along with the other fellows in stealing an automobile; it was so easy and such a hilarious joke on all the "squares." Besides, he was afraid of these other fellows, especially big Sam whom they all seemed to admire. Stealing the car was easy. It was also easy for the police to find out all about it. Rusty now has a "police record" and he is amazed and also a little frightened because his parents are so unhappy and so stern. He wonders if they really love him any more. Perhaps big Sam is right and all parents can be ignored because they are "square." And yet that thought does not bring Rusty much satisfaction. He is unhappy, too.

In meeting this particular challenge of life, Rusty might have used judgment by asking some questions: What are the consequences of breaking a law, whether or not I am caught? How may this adventure affect my parents, other people, my own future, even the whole community in which I live? Suppose all parents *are* square; are they not also people like me? How would I feel in their place? So, I don't like this town I live in, and want to do something to show I don't like it. But is that the whole story? Are my personal feelings about things all that matter? Is there anything I can do to make the town a pleasanter place to be?

In asking himself these questions, Rusty is considering in one particular situation what it means to be a human person, one who is free and responsible, and endowed with reason and imagination. He is considering what to do in the light of principles and values.

In this particular instance, Rusty may not have had time to think and to consider all such questions. He might, then, have walked out on the situation. In this case, he would be risking big Sam's displeasure. Rusty may feel that being at outs with big Sam is more than he can take. If so, Rusty is no longer a free human being; he has allowed big Sam to make him a slave, that is, one who is not allowed to decide anything for himself because he is controlled by another person. Perhaps Rusty was so overwhelmed by the whole situation that he was unable to think at all, but could only act according to Sam's orders.

Although these are possible reasons that may explain Rusty's lack of judgment, they are not excuses for it. The person who participates fully in life, affirming his existence as a free and responsible human being, does not surrender his judgment in any situation. Always he recognizes the human framework of existence. This means he is connected with other people who must be taken into account. Believing himself to be a child of God, he considers the meaning of this relationship in every challenge of life.

MEETING LIFE'S OPPORTUNITIES AND RESPONSIBILITIES

In addition to the challenges of adventure, and the need to say "No," life offers us opportunities for work, service, and play. These three types of experiences cover most of any person's lifelong activities. Each comes with its particular built-in responsibilities.

71

1. Work to Be Done

At present most of your work has to do with your occupation as a student: reading, writing papers, doing problems in math or experiments in chemistry, developing a project in English or the arts, participating in classroom work, taking examinations, joining in the life of the high school community. What is the meaning of work in this situation?

Let's say you have thought you would like to go to college but the family income cannot pay for it. Let's say further that you apply for and are granted a substantial scholarship. This is wonderful, and there is joy all round. But are you "home free"? No. This scholarship presents an opportunity for which you are appropriately joyful, but it also brings with it an obligation or responsibility. Fulfilling this obligation means working as a student to the best of your ability.

Taking on this responsibility does not mean that you must necessarily try for a straight-A academic record. This may not be a realistic goal for you. It does mean not being lax in your studies, and not being careless about class assignments. It will likely mean saying "no" at times to a momentary or even long-lasting pleasure, because the responsibility you have accepted must have a priority in your schedule. You do not have to be grim about this obligation, nor turn yourself into a grind. There are also play and service opportunities in every well-rounded life. In going to college on a scholarship you are making daily decisions in light of principles or values we have discussed and which you believe represent God's purpose for you.

One of the dividends we receive from meeting life's opportunities is the chance to learn how to take responsibility easily (that is, in our stride) as well as seriously. Assuming a task, short or long term, and putting our best energy and inventiveness into it, being faithful in following it to conclusion, is a very satisfying experience. Persons may begin at a very early age to learn how to assume responsibility and to sense the rewards it brings. But if they have not had that opportunity early, they may begin it at any age. Instead of feeling tricked because life's opportunities also imply responsibilities, we may feel good about the additional satisfaction involved. At the same time, we recognize the demands of self-discipline and self-denial that are also involved.

The situation of the student accepting the scholarship is similar to many situations in the world of work that will arise throughout your life. To be engaged in work, either physical, mental, or both, to have a job to do that has meaning for you and calls forth your powers as a person, brings out the richness of life in which you are a free and responsible participant. Many times work experiences bring us in touch with varied and interesting people, with engrossing new skills and enlarging ideas.

Our work may have this quality whether or not we are paid for it. In every person's life there is much work for which he is not paid. We can almost say that the satisfaction that work brings has little to do with the payment received. Almost, but not quite. It makes a great difference in the world of work, in the economic ordering of our society, whether or not persons receive adequate pay for the jobs they perform. This question, however, has to do with economic justice. It is separate from, though related to, the question of personal satisfactions derived from one's work.

It has been true in the past, though it is less true today, that many people perform jobs that do not provide opportunity for personal growth and satisfaction. These jobs narrow life, impair health, degrade personality. Work of this kind has been associated with some types of coal mining, farming, manufacturing, merchandizing, domestic service. We must recognize this fact so that we do not claim that all work represents an opportunity to affirm the good things of life. We must recognize too, that it is often not the job itself which degrades but the conditions under which the job must be performed. Digging coal, picking beets, running a sewing machine in a factory, or mopping a floor may bring many of the satisfactions suggested above, provided the working conditions tend to support them and there is a purpose in doing them which lifts the work beyond drudgery. Even though the working conditions of all jobs are not yet what they should be, progress has been made in recent years with the use of machines to take on the tasks of routine drudgery, and especially the enactment of laws regulating working conditions.

2. Play to Be Enjoyed

In one sense we can say that play is the opposite of work. In another sense we can say that there is only a thin line between what is work and what is play. It is helpful, however, to make a real distinction between the two in order to sort out the opportunities of life, and to know how to choose among them in the light of principles and values we accept.

Play is any activity which brings diversion from life's routines, involves a person voluntarily, and which is engaged in for pleasure in itself alone and not for some end beyond itself. For example, a neighborhood game of softball or tennis or badminton would be play for the participants. On the other hand, a professional game of ice hockey would be work for the participants. The ice hockey team is working and not playing because they are using the game not for itself alone but for a living. That example is easy to see. Another one less easy to see might be: making decorations to transform the gym for the senior dance would be work. Taking pictures at the dance for your memory book would be play. Here we see that fine line but also the distinction. Making the decorations was fun! But a lot of work is fun. Taking the pictures was also fun. So are they the same? No, because the decorations are to serve a purpose beyond themselves, that is, to make the gym look different. The pictures are to serve a purpose *in* themselves, that is, to recall a good time.

There is another difference between these two activities, both of which were fun. Making the decorations was work because they had to be made according to a pre-determined plan and completed by a certain time if their purpose is to be carried out. A work situation nearly always imposes restrictions that cut down on the chance to be spontaneous. Play, on the other hand, is freer. We are not bound by as many restrictions when we play. We are free to begin, or to stop. We can decide whether or not to take the pictures; we can try to take "good" pictures or we are free not to bother with the rules of good photography and snap pictures casually.

One of the fine opportunities life offers us is spontaneous play of our own choosing. The essence of play is enjoyment for its own sake. When we see play in this way, we recognize that it is quite different from work, although each one may bring satisfaction and may require more or less effort. We see also that work and play can produce an alternating rhythm in life. The discipline of work takes turns with the spontaneity of play. Both kinds of opportunities are important in life. Either without the other would likely become dreary.

Sometimes people turn play into work; then the satisfactions of play are short-circuited. Some high school basketball teams play not so much for the enjoyment of the game as to make a reputation for their school, to add to its prestige in sports. They have turned play into work by making it serve an end beyond itself. We should not turn play into work, nor should we allow our own play to cut off the opportunities of play for other people. If Alice stays at Emily's house listening to records so late that she cannot help her mother prepare the family's dinner, possibly she is depriving her mother of leisure-time opportunity.

There are almost as many different kinds of play as there are people. In fact, because play is so free, we can often tell a lot about a person through what he does for play. These are the activities he chooses for himself and the way he spends his free time.

There is the boy who plays chess, a game that requires rigorous, intellectual concentration and effort. Here is another who makes a game of collecting bottle caps to find the lucky number. Here is a family who is building a canoe to enjoy in the neighboring waterways, a project requiring extended effort and skill. Here is a girl who enjoys sitting on a rocky beach watching the variety of animal life going about its business in the water and the sand. Another girl likes to be more with people, reveling in the play of conversation and banter. Yet another prefers the combo. One boy likes a hard game of handball; another likes a book on a stimulating topic; another likes puzzles; and still another likes a walk in the city streets. One person may enjoy many forms of play, while another may not yet recognize the joys genuine play can bring him.

3. SERVICE TO BE PERFORMED

Life's myriad opportunities for work and play suggest that, quite literally, we are here to work and to play.

God's purpose in life for us, however, is not completed in these opportunities. What are we here for? Not just for ourselves but also for other people. In addition to work and play, life offers us opportunities for freely given service—those activities through which we enter into the lives of others, sharing their too-heavy loads or their suffering, or relieving loneliness, or offering friendly support in temptation, or ministering to their physical need.

All of us are naturally self-centered. We have an inborn tendency to think primarily of what we want, what serves our interest, and to wish to be first and best. Each of us also is of worth. It is important that each of us live his life to the full. But in order to live life to the full, we find that we must strive also to rise above exclusive concern for ourselves and to include other persons in our concern. Only so can we be really happy. The reason lies in the basic understanding that apart from one another we are not whole persons. Since we share with others in God's care, so we are made to have concern for one another. Loving others as we love ourselves is our response to God's love for us.

Opportunities to act upon this concern are all about us. We see them in our day-by-day experience at points where decisions are called for. Most of our work and play activities involve us in human relationships of many kinds—with family, friends, teammates, classmates, neighbors, casual acquaintances, as well as with those people everywhere to whom we are related as human persons but never see face to face. These relationships with people offer channels for sharing life's joys and responsibilities.

To understand and help another person requires patience, imagination, and sustained interest. Many of the "kindnesses" people extend to one another—the bowl of soup to the sick neighbor, the loan of a skirt, the help with the algebra problem, the ride to school—are good social conventions but they are not what is meant by service. These conventions may or may not be helpful to the recipient, and in any case they are often motivated primarily by a wish to do what one is expected to do, rather than a real concern for the other person.

To be truly helpful to someone, we must first understand what *he* thinks will be helpful to him. Such understanding requires the imagination to put ourselves in his shoes, to see how his situation must look to him at this moment. Perhaps the sick neighbor does not regard the bowl of soup as particularly helpful. She would, however, be truly served by having someone take her three-year-old off her hands for a while. So out of your concern for your neighbor, you offer to take Billy to the park. You had intended to work on your stamp collection or to go to the "Y" to bowl, but right across your side yard a neighbor needs your help.

Similarly, when you begin to use your imagination you see that Linda does not need your skirt; what she really needs is companionship. Can you be inventive in finding ways to include her in some of your activities? This may be hard. Perhaps Linda is not very attractive or responsive; she isn't much fun to be with; your other friends may think you are wasting your time. Genuine concern for Linda's welfare, however, will call upon your patience and sustained interest. It will stimulate your imagination to come up with some new ways of relating Linda to your friends.

In service to others we must accept the possibility of not knowing whether we have been truly helpful in a particular situation even after doing our best. Some persons do not and others cannot express appreciation in an adequate way. That does not mean necessarily that these persons are not aware of and grateful for our help. Indeed, sometimes we are most helpful when the person we help does *not* know it. The helpful relationship between persons is never a bargain. We expect nothing in return. In fact, if the person receiving the service assumes he must "pay back" the giver, the experience is more like a trade than an act of service. There are times when such trading is appropriate in human relationships, but trading is not what is meant by service.

Just as we are willing to help other persons freely, without interest in return or reward, we should be equally willing to accept acts of service from other people. One of the temptations that beset some persons is their unwillingness to admit that they also need help. Rather subtly such a person begins to feel superior and perhaps arrogant in what he thinks is his independence. In actual fact, no one of us is so independent and self-reliant that he does not need help from others. A few moments' thought will make clear to each of us how much we depend upon the work and love of other persons. We are all interdependent in our human relationships. One of the marks of being children of God is that we freely and responsibly and joyously both give and receive help from one another without "counting the cost" or expecting any reward.

So far we have explored opportunities for showing interest and concern for people with whom we are in personal contact. Our opportunity and responsibility, however, do not stop at the edge of our immediate circle. We live also in the much larger circle of God's children everywhere.

When we think imaginatively of the many people everywhere, we recognize that one of the needs of many persons is expansion of their opportunities. When we think clearly and honestly, we know that most of our own opportunities come to us not because we are especially worthy or because we have earned them, but because someone else has loved us and worked for us. In a similar way it happens that life does not present opportunities for either work or play to some people, not because of what they themselves have done or left undone, but because of conditions over which they have very little control. This is especially true at present of persons in the late teens and early twenties without adequate schooling. Often they have dropped out of school because they did not have decent clothes or a place to study or anyone to encourage them or to expect anything of them. They do not have opportunities for work, not only of the kind that brings personal satisfaction, but any kind of work which could support them. There is little these people can do by themselves in our society to improve their situation. Jobs require qualifications they simply do not have and are unable to acquire. So every day they sink deeper into hopelessness and despair.

This social situation in our society presents other people with an important obligation to try to change the conditions. This may begin with direct action in keeping the younger children in such discouraged families from falling into the same pattern. Perhaps some member of your family is helping in a tutoring program for girls and boys who are likely to drop out of school unless they can get help which neither the schools nor their families can give. Sometimes the effort to change conditions is indirect, through the giving of money to provide needed assistance, or through the enactment of helpful laws supported by the payment of taxes.

Housing conditions in some areas seriously limit the opportunities for play, denying some people healthful and invigorating experiences. As children of God we accept the obligation of rendering service in these areas, direct and indirect.

When with the support of others and through changed conditions, these persons find and accept opportunities for work and play, they also accept the obligations of showing concern for others. Work, play, concern and service for others—all three are needed in the lives of all persons so they may participate in life freely and responsibly as children of God.

BEING FAITHFUL TO GOD

Remember Chuck? We left him scowling at his baby brother in the playpen. We do not know how Chuck would find his answer to the questions he was asking, but he might have reflected along these lines:

Life is basically good and not bad because God has made it that way. Therefore this business of staying here with John instead of being with Ted can't be as black as I'm making it seem.

"Well, what is there in it?" asks Chuck. "What can I make out of this job I'm stuck with?"

This simple inquiry takes Chuck's attention off himself and on to the baby. As he watches John for a few minutes with his mind as well as his eyes, Chuck sees that the baby is busily trying to pull himself upright by grabbing the top rail of the playpen. With a big effort he finally manages to stand on his two feet, wobbling but holding securely on the rail. Chuck smiles broadly and walks over to John.

"Good for you, joker," he says.

John laughs out loud with delight over the approving tone in his brother's voice and with enjoyment of his own achievement. But he forgets to keep hold of the rail and falls backward with a slight thump, and starts to cry.

"Look here, John," Chuck says, "let's try that again." He picks the baby up, sets him firmly on his bottom, putting his hands on the rail. "Now pull hard."

If Chuck were to reflect on the time spent with John that afternoon, he might have seen it as one of life's minor challenges. Because he had not paid much attention to the baby since his arrival, Chuck did not know John. In fact, the whole idea of babyhood was unknown territory. The experience of having a baby brother in the family was something to be explored—an experience that might offer satisfying opportunities for work, play, and service. To decide to enter the experience with that attitude is to be faithful to one's promise to God to live in accord with his purpose, participating freely and responsibly in all of life's challenges—small as well as large.

4.

WHAT WILL
I BECOME?

YOUTH is a special time of becoming. As you move through the teen years you are aware of becoming taller, stronger, more like an adult in the way your body is developing. You are becoming more aware of the world outside your parents' home, your school, church, neighborhood. You are becoming conscious of your own ideas about things; and perhaps you are feeling strongly that you should make more of your own decisions. Mother's notions about clothes and what it means to have a good time, and father's rules about when you must be home and when you will be able to drive the car, may strike you as inappropriate to what you are becoming. At the same time you are often puzzled and uncertain about what these experiences of "becoming" mean. These wonderments may be summed up in the question: What is my future to be?

SOME PUZZLES ABOUT THE FUTURE

Lately Peter has been wondering quite a lot about his future—ever since he read that piece in the paper about his father. The newspaper reported some important medical research going on at the local university which would make a major contribution to community health. The story mentioned the fine work of Peter's father in connection with that research. Peter knew his father was a research scientist in medicine, but he had not thought before of the real point of his father's work. Now his thoughts ran something like this: Sure, his father was a "nice guy," but maybe he was more than that, maybe he was really "great" because the results of his work would be helpful to so many people. Will I be like my father when I grow up? Is helping people a part of the kind of job you do? But I don't even like science. So Peter was wondering.

Marilyn buried her head in the pillow so nobody would hear that she was crying. The voices of her mother and father rose harsh and angry through the closed door. Marilyn felt she could not stand it any longer. Why did her parents fight so much? She knew from other times that her mother's face would be pained and bitter, and that her father would look hard and stony. Why does life have to be this way? Is this what marriage is like? Will my marriage be this way? So Marilyn, too, wonders about the future in a kind of agony.

Dorothy is picturing the future, too, but in a different mood. She has just finished a novel about the life of a nurse. Maybe that's what I will become, she thinks. In her mind she sees herself in a chic white uniform with a perky cap pinned becomingly on top of her smooth hair. As Dorothy's imagination gains speed, she sees her slim figure moving from bed to bed with a pat and a smile for all the patients, who smile back and murmur appreciation. Yes, says Dorothy to herself, that's what I want to become.

Mike hangs up the telephone and slumps against the wall. He has just told Joe that he can't go to camp this summer because his parents can't afford it. The disappointment breaks over him in a great wave. The final "no" to his hopes is harder to take because he can't be angry with his parents. He knows exactly what his father is able to earn; he knows the struggle his mother has to stretch the modest sum over the family's needs. In fact, he thinks his mother and father are the nicest people he knows. All the same, there is not enough money. It's as simple as that. And always has been. How many times, Mike asks himself, have I had to go without important things just because there isn't enough money? Money, and a lot of it, must be necessary in life because so much seems to depend on it. Okay, thinks Mike, what I'm going to do is to make a lot of money. The disappointment begins to recede a little as Mike tries to figure what he must do to prepare himself for becoming a big money-maker.

Tony, on the other hand, hardly wonders about his future; he is sure there won't be any future for him. One bright spring day he sits on the end of the pier with his feet hanging over the dirty water of the river and watches the ferry chugging across to the other side. He knows he shouldn't be there, but he figures it will be fifteen minutes at least before a cop or one of the dockmen notices him. He doesn't much care, anyway. They always tell him to stop hanging around, to go home. The last place, really the last, that Tony wants to go is home. Home is very clear in Tony's mind. It's dirty and noisy with crying kids. He'd have to fight the rats to get to the door of his mother's two rooms in the cold-water flat. The main thing Tony wants is to leave home—anything to get away. So he left school and started looking for work in order to be on his own. This very afternoon he had been told again that without a high school diploma and with his "background" there wasn't a chance. His "background"? He knew there was an ugly word that described his mother, but what did that have to do with him? Yet everywhere he turned there was a dead end. So the future was closed, he told himself, there was no exit. He wondered what it would be like to slip off the pier and let the chill waters of the river carry him out to sea.

Red is sure there is a future for him. His carrot-colored crew cut stood up straight and bushy as he put two big bags of groceries into the customer's car. "Thank you, Mrs. Greene," he said, "I'll phone you as soon as those raspberries come in from Mr. Paoli's farm." Back inside the store Red looked around. No customers seemed to need him, and even the vegetables were still in good order since he had arranged them an hour ago. His father was taking an order over the phone in an easy, warm voice. Red loves his father's grocery store. He likes its friendly atmosphere, the neat and colorful stacks of merchandise, the nice customers. He had done small chores around the place ever since he could remember. Now that he is in high school he is beginning to learn some of the essentials of the business, including those special services which made many shoppers prefer his father's independent grocery to the supermarket. Red wants to go to work in the store full time as soon as he finishes high school, but his father insists on college. When Red thinks of the future he knows that what he most wants is to carry on his father's business.

THE PRESENT: FROM THE PAST INTO THE FUTURE

Whenever we think about the future we must at the same time think about the present and the past, because present, past, and future are very closely related. Part of who, what, and where you are today depends upon decisions made and actions taken in the past not only by your parents and grandparents but also by persons in the long-ago past of whom you have never heard. Part of what you will become, of your future, is decided by what you do now in the present.

In a sense there is only the present, because we bring forward the past into the present and also because "tomorrow" never comes. Therefore, when we imagine what our future will be like, what we will become, we are actually taking a point of view toward the present. When we try to look into the future, we imagine it in terms of what we know about the present. Sometimes we want the future to be continuous with the present. That is Red's view. He sees his future as growing directly out of the present. He might describe this future as more of the same only much more so.

Sometimes we want the future to be different from the present. We long for a definite break with the present as we see it. This is Tony's overwhelming desire. As long as his present continues, he sees his future completely blocked. Marilyn, too, has difficulty in viewing her own future except as she sees her present. Because her present circumstances are painful, she is afraid the future will be painful, too.

To see the past in the present, and to view the future in terms of the present, is the experience of living in history and seeing ourselves as a part of history. This includes not only our personal history but social history, that is, the lives of whole peoples; for example, the Americans, or the Arabs, or the Polynesians of the South Pacific. Each of us has a social history related to the "people" to whom we belong. In our present world the histories of whole peoples are intertwined, so that the present and future of one people are tied up with the present and future of most other peoples.

To think about what you will become is to have some beginning ideas about your personal destiny. Or to say it another way: Reflecting on the future is imagining what life will be like, what it will amount to. The way a person views his destiny is important because it influences his action in the present, which in turn will in some way be carried forward into the future.

SOME VIEWS OF HOW THE FUTURE COMES TO BE

Persons have varied views of destiny. For example, some people think the destiny of all of us is determined by something outside ourselves, perhaps God, or the force of circumstances, or sheer accident or chance. Therefore one's destiny can only be accepted and endured, not changed. What is going to happen, will happen, and there's no use in concerning ourselves about it.

Other people take the opposite view. They believe that people can in large measure control their destiny, and mold life just the way they want it. Still other people think that destiny is unimportant or even meaningless. In this view, the future doesn't matter; you just live from day to day.

You can see how each of these ideas about destiny, that is, what determines how a person's life will add up in the future, will influence that person's actions, feelings, decisions in the present life.

There is still another view of destiny, however. In this view destiny is related to God's purpose for all his children. We have already seen how religious faith affirms that because of God's purpose in creation life has meaning; gradually it can be understood; persons can participate in life enjoyably, responsibly, and significantly. Therefore, when persons accept this view they can think about their future with confidence and make plans for the days and years ahead.

To have a part in influencing our future is not the same thing as controlling our destiny, that is, making sure that our future will be exactly the way we want it to be. So many things in life are outside our control that we can never be absolutely certain about the future. For example, Red's future looks fairly certain. But suppose his father dies before Red is out of high school and his mother has to sell his father's business? These circumstances would change Red's future considerably, although he might still be able to carry out some of his present plans.

Tony doesn't see that he has any future because he feels trapped in his present unfavorable circumstances. But suppose a person comes into Tony's life who is able to help him return to school with better preparation and with changed ideas about his school experience, and so offer an avenue of progress from his present life?

Events at present unforeseen will cause changes in the external circumstances of our lives and also changes in ourselves. We can influence to some extent what the specific changes will be by the attitude we take toward the event. Red may take the attitude that his whole future is lost because he will be unable to carry on his father's business. Or he may take the attitude that he must change a part of his plans for the future but not give up the basic idea of what he wants to do. Tony may take the attitude that nothing can change his experiences or his ideas in relation to school, or he may be willing to respond to the interest and ideas of another person, and change his own views enough to make another try.

We do play a definite part in determining our destiny, although we cannot control the future. If we believe that God has a purpose for us as his children, we know that this purpose may be fulfilled in many ways. We do not demand that it be fulfilled in the one particular way we may see at the moment. We know we are not wise enough, so we trust God to help us grow in understanding of his purposes as new experiences come from year to year. Making our plans for the future in this expectation will make our lives more meaningful. We have confidence our destiny may be significant regardless of the external circumstances which we meet in life.

THE IMPORTANCE OF YOUR FUTURE

In the framework of this Christian view of destiny, what are the ways we may think about what we will become? How may we take account of the past, live fully in the present, and look confidently to the future?

Let's affirm at once that what each of us becomes matters. It matters to God who loves, cares for, and guides every one of his children. Our future matters to other people, and to the world. Perhaps you may think that the world couldn't care less about what you become. Even the persons in your immediate circle—parents, friends, teachers—may seem to you indifferent about your future. They do not listen to your dreams and plans, or their lack of concern makes you hesitate to speak of your ideas about your future. Or again, your parents may have such a firm idea about what they want you to become that they seem to lack interest in your own ideas. You may or may not be interpreting accurately the attitudes of these other people, but in either case your future does matter to them. Your future is tied up with the futures of most of the persons in your immediate circle.

Beyond this circle of your personal life is the world at large to which your future matters very much. The world needs persons who dream creatively and constructively about their future. The world needs persons who care about other people, who are willing to work to understand the natural world and to find ways by which persons and nations can live together in peace.

Our future also matters to ourselves. What we think, feel, and do today will show up in results or consequences tomorrow—"tomorrow" in the short run meaning the next day, or "tomorrow" in the long run meaning a more distant time. It matters whether we live life to the full or live it meagerly; whether we realize all our capacities or only a small part of them.

Some persons seem to believe that the future does not matter to them. Those who view destiny as meaningless or completely beyond control are in this group. But also in this group are many more people who cannot imagine anything beyond the present day, or who cannot muster the patience to wait or accept the discipline of making decisions. We all may act like this at some time.

For example, a person may decide to go to a dance even though ill with a cold and fever—this action says that the future does not count. The fact that this action may result in several days or weeks of serious illness is either not taken into account, or is considered unimportant compared with missing the immediate satisfactions of the dance. A person may buy an attractive shirt on impulse with money he had earlier decided to save in order to buy a camera. This action also says the future doesn't count. If repeated, this decision may delay getting the camera indefinitely. Some students act as if the future doesn't matter when they do not take their studies seriously until the day of examination is close at hand. A few students never take their studies seriously, and thus critically limit what they will be able to become in the future. The same is true of the few students who take their studies over-seriously and neglect play and concern and service for others.

The difference between people who recognize that the future counts, and those who don't, is that the persons in the first group are able or willing to ask themselves, "What if?" "If I do this, or don't do it, or do something else, *what* is likely to happen, both today and tomorrow, in each case?" In other words, these people try to foresee consequences because they know the future matters.

YOUR GOALS AND YOUR FUTURE

Making decisions brings up the subject of goals, because any serious decision is made according to the goals you have in mind. Your goals are important because you will likely become in the future what your goals are in the present. Thus in reflecting on your future you may well take a clear-eyed look at your goals.

1. WHERE DO GOALS COME FROM?

A person does not just suddenly come up with goals. What he wants to be and to achieve in life grows out of his association with other persons, his own experiences, and what has been called the experience of the race. That is, what men have learned through the years and have summarized in history, in literature, in art, and in the record of their experience of God's revelation of his purposes. It is the record of man's experience of God's revelation of his purposes which is most important within the scope of this book. For we are affirming the faith that God is making his purposes known to his children, and that to understand and fulfill these purposes is to enable a person to live life to the full, confidently, and joyfully. And so, in seeking to set our goals, we wish them to be in harmony with God's good purposes.

We have reviewed in Chapter Three what Jesus taught men about these purposes. We have seen how these teachings offer us principles and values for our lives. They also are the source of the life goals which the experiences of persons have shown to be the most satisfying.

There will be many short-term specific goals in your life. There will be goals of many different sorts—school goals, friendship goals, athletic goals, and the like. But back of them all will be your over-all life goals. And against these you will check all the short-term, specific goals. In this way your life will hold together and move forward with meaning.

Let us now think about our more specific goals and try to understand how we may set them and how we may test and evaluate them and revise them. First, it is important to be able to recognize unconscious or unreal goals.

2. WHEN GOALS ARE NOT REAL

What would you say was Dorothy's goal—the girl who imagined herself a nurse? Was it to be a nurse, or was it to be attractive and admired? Probably Dorothy was unaware of what her real goal was. Perhaps she was merely dreaming about herself, and was not being serious about her future. In any case, Dorothy's apparent goal was both unconscious and unrealistic.

Her goal was unrealistic because she had a false picture of what a nurse really does. Nursing involves standing on your feet for many hours, sometimes lifting or turning heavy patients, performing for patients chores that are often considered "dirty," offensive, or menial. Most nurses are so busy while on duty that they do not have time to consider whether or not they are "attractive" in appearance.

On the other hand, nursing is a profession that can be of great service to people in an immediate and direct way. It is true that a nurse often has opportunity to bring help, relief, and comfort to persons who are in dire need of these services. It is a mistake, however, to imagine as Dorothy did that all people will always appreciate these services.

Dorothy's dreaming reminds us that in setting goals for the future we must be as accurate as possible about what the realization of the goal will require.

3. Goals That Are Your Own

Let's look at Peter's goal. It is somewhat vague and certainly more complex than Dorothy's. He evidently wants to be a "great" man like his father but is doubtful about it because he does not "like science" which is his father's field of work.

We can get two helpful clues from Peter's situation. The first one is that a person's goals should be appropriate to the kind of person he is. If we recall what was said in Chapter Two about who we are, we recognize that each person has special capacities and limitations. When setting goals for ourselves we should take into account these special characteristics. It may be that Peter does not like science because he has little capacity for it. Therefore, it would be foolish for him to think of becoming a scientist like his father.

The second clue we find in Peter's situation is that our goals should be our own, not those of someone else. Peter is close to taking over his father's goal instead of setting up his own goal. People are often tempted to try to imitate those whom they admire. Imitation of another person is an acknowledgement that a person does not yet know who he is; his self-understanding is quite limited. To come to know yourself is to accept yourself as an individual, different from others in many ways, and to be willing to be yourself, choosing goals and making decisions appropriate to you.

Does this mean that Peter cannot be a "great" man like his father? Not at all. There are many ways of being "great," especially in making a significant contribution to human life. And there are many ways of expressing admiration for a person, of learning from him, and of being helped by the quality of his life, none of which includes imitation.

One of the encouraging facts about the willingness to be yourself is that you are not *bound* to be like someone else. Just because someone close to you has certain goals does not mean you must have them, too. Take Marilyn, for instance. We do not know what her parents' goals are, but their behavior indicates that their goal is to exert power over each other, and each wants to assert himself at the expense of the other. Such goals usually lead to tough conflicts that are destructive to both parties. Marilyn, however, is not bound by such self-destructive goals if she is willing to be Marilyn and not a copy of either parent. Thus she can be assured that all marriage is not like that in her home, and also that she is free to set for herself different goals of relationship with other persons that likely will lead to marriage of a different kind.

4. When Goals Are in Conflict

Sometimes our personal goals are in conflict with one another, forcing us to choose among them. Life often presents us with short-term goals in competition with long-term goals. This is the case noted above of the shirt versus the camera, and going to the dance versus health. The reason such competition between goals makes a problem for us is that the short-term choice nearly always seems more *immediately* rewarding. Here is some object or some experience we want very much because it will bring satisfaction almost at once. The satisfaction of the long-term goal often is longer delayed (buying the camera) or not quite real at the moment (not having to miss out of future activities because of illness). It is probable that Red faces this competition between a short-term and long-term goal. Going to college for sounder preparation for life is a long-term goal; going full-time into his father's business upon graduation from high school is a short-term goal.

Thus we are faced with the problem of weighing goals against each other to decide which one is most important to us in terms of the way we see our future, what we want to become. It is not always true that the long-term goal is the better choice. It is equally true that every person who takes his future seriously must learn sometimes to delay a present good for the sake of a future greater good; in other words, to say "no," sometimes, to short-term satisfactions.

5. Understanding the Meaning of a Goal

One more important point about goals in life is that we must be as sure as we can be about the meaning of a particular goal. We can often get at the meaning of a goal by asking: If I work toward this goal and really attain it, will

I accomplish what I want to accomplish? It may be that Mike will never ask that question about his goal of making a lot of money until the day comes, possibly much later in life, when he has acquired the money to buy the kind of thing he now wants. On that day he may realize that he wants even more some things in life that money will not buy. He may also realize that by working very hard toward the goal of acquiring money he has missed the value of some other goals. This meaning, however, will not be clear to Mike while he is in the mood of disappointment over missing something he now wants. It is also hard for him to grasp this meaning because so much of his experience is having to "do without." If in some way Mike could enlarge his experience so that he could get a wider perspective on exactly what kind of satisfaction money will bring, and what ones it will not bring, he could better decide whether money-making is the goal he wants. Also he would be helped by trying to foresee what he will have to do and what he will have to give up to attain such a goal.

There are ways that Mike can enlarge his understanding. One way is to look all around a possible goal, not just on one side of it. At the moment when we saw Mike he was looking at only one side of "having a lot of money." He wanted to go to camp. When he is calmer, he may be able to walk around and look at another side. For instance, he lives in a family in which there are respect and understanding among the members. He loves and admires his parents, who love and care for him. This is a relationship that he values very much and in which he finds deep satisfaction. He values it especially when he remembers his friends who do not enjoy this kind of family life. Probably he knows someone like Marilyn. Looking on this side of his goal, he can see that "having a lot of money" will not necessarily bring loving family relationships. So Mike might conclude that money isn't what is most important to him. "Look what I have without it!"

But there is still another side of this goal to be considered. Whereas Mike's family does not have enough money for many things he wants, they apparently are not living in poverty. His father's earnings provide the necessities. Income does matter, even in the building of loving relationships. When persons live in real poverty, they are often so hard-pressed that the experience of love is almost impossible. Tony seems to be in just that situation. From his point of view, living in deep deprivation, Mike's family may seem to have "a lot of money." So it seems that a goal to have a reasonable amount of money is necessary for people in our society, to have a good life. But there is a sharp limitation on the satisfactions additional large amounts will provide. When Mike's goal is viewed from several angles in this way, we see its meaning becoming clearer. This is true of any goal.

6. CHOOSING GOALS

Some questions to ask in choosing a goal, either short-term or long-term, are: What is its value in comparison with other goals? What will be the result of working toward this goal?

One way to get at the answers to these questions is to look at a possible goal for our lives in the light of who we are and the purpose of our lives. Is this goal appropriate for my life as a human being of dignity and worth, a child of God? Does it support me as a free and responsible person or does it undermine my freedom and make me an irresponsible person? Does it enable me to live in love with others, or does it put me in conflict with my neighbor?

Let's begin by considering some short-term goals which contribute to life's over-all goals. For example, there is a club to which you would like to belong because the members are people whom you admire and with whom you would like to be associated. Membership in this club would help your social life; you believe it would be fun. Perhaps your immediate goal is to be invited to join this club. Before accepting this goal, however, you might take a look at what membership in this club may involve. Ask such questions as these: What controls over my life will this club have? What are the spoken or unspoken rules among the members? Some clubs put heavy pressure on their members about the friends they have who are not members, about the amount of money they spend, about the kinds of activities they may or may not engage in. In other words, some clubs try to take away some of the freedom of their members to make their own choices. They exert this control through social pressure, that is, making the member feel unaccepted and unwanted if he does not conform to these rules.

When considering the goal of belonging to this club it

is a good idea to discover whether or not you would have to submit to this kind of control, and, if so, to consider whether or not this kind of conformity is appropriate for you as a free and responsible child of God. Would it mean, for instance, that you would be expected to treat some other human beings as not worthy of your respect and friendship? You might also consider the opportunities for work, play, and service offered by the club's program. Are they the kind of opportunities that you believe to be in harmony with God's purpose for his children?

You may discover from all this questioning that the findings are reasonably positive and so you feel good about accepting membership. Or, on the other hand, you may find so many negative possibilities that the goal of membership in this club no longer seems as desirable as it did at first.

Another set of questions to ask in choosing goals is: Is this goal a real possibility for me? Given my situation and capacities, will I be likely to attain it? What will it cost both me and others in money, effort, and time? It is important to weigh the cost in effort and time as well as money. Take the goal of a college education which requires all three. This decision faces many high school students, and usually must be made some time, often years, in advance of graduation. Also this decision is correlated directly to personal interests, capacities, and resources.

In order for the years of college experience to be valuable and enriching, the student must consciously and on his own choose this goal. He must not be pushed either into or away from college by outside pressure from parents, friends, or high school advisors. He will need the information and counsel he receives from these persons, but he must not allow them to make the final decision for him.

So, during the high school years, you may be thinking about such questions as these and acquiring the information that will help you arrive at some answers: Am I interested in going to college? Why or why not? If so, what kind of college education would be most congenial and beneficial to me? If not, what are the alternatives? Trade school? Trade apprenticeship? Marriage? An immediate job? What are my interests and capacities that would be influential in making this decision? What financial resources are required for college? What are required for some alternative? What must I do now and in the immediate future in case I choose college as a goal? In case I do not choose college? In either case, what are the likely short-term and long-term results? In each case, am I willing to undertake the cost in time, work, money?

Sometimes young people decide on college as a goal because all their friends are going or because their parents have this kind of ambition for them, and not because they are genuinely interested or consider it an appropriate and congenial goal. In that case, paying the cost becomes extremely difficult and the college experience may be unrewarding, or may result in failure. It is possible also that some young people decide against college because their parents or others discourage them even though they are interested in a college education and are willing to pay the cost. In that case, the young people may suffer major frustrations for many years.

In all situations a young person should try hard to summon the necessary courage, and to marshal the arguments and the facts that will enable him to make his own decision—to choose his own goal. It is not always possible to bring off such a decision, but often it is more possible than young people think it is. Difficulties which sometimes loom as impossible to overcome, often are overcome when one has a clearly defined goal of his own.

You can see that choosing a significant long-term goal requires thought and information and time enough to look at it from many angles. You should try to get as much help as you can, and to ask some of the hard questions, and then make up your own mind.

7. Working Toward a Goal

When you have taken care in choosing a goal, you have, in fact, taken a long step in working toward achieving it. You have tried to predict what may be expected and you have assessed your capacities that will help you attain it.

Again let us get perspective from short-term goals. If your goal is knitting a sweater for your boy friend for Christmas, you have calculated the cost of yarn, how many hours of your time will probably be required, and you have some idea of where you will get those hours in your time schedule before the Christmas Eve deadline. If your goal is to learn how to be skillful with a surf board, you have estimated the amount of practice and instruction it will take, and the opportunities you will have for using the surf board. If the goal is to learn to play the saxophone or to lose twenty-five pounds, or to make straight A's this school semester, you will decide why you want to achieve it and what it will require.

Any one of these goals requires sustained effort. The ability to "stick with it," to make yourself keep on when you want to quit, is a requirement for these specific goals. It is also a requirement for achieving any significant long-term goal.

If your goal is to learn how to manage your temper better in order not to fly off the handle so often, you realize that it will require discipline involving being more relaxed, holding your tongue, putting your attention on the other fellow instead of your own feelings. If your goal is to try to understand your mother so that you will get along with her more happily, you are ready to put out what it takes—planning to be more responsible about the house, listening to her especially when she talks about her interests, letting her actions that annoy you go by without an angry response from you.

The ability to stick with a goal may be acquired. One way of acquiring this ability is to put your attention on the goal—why you decided on it in the first place—instead of giving in to all of the occasional impulses that will slow down or even prevent your achievement. The casual impulse that hits you suddenly is often the enemy of sustained effort. So don't give in to an impulse too quickly before

you have had time to think about the possible consequences it may have.

Your sustained effort also is strengthened by taking one
step at a time, and working on that step before looking
forward to the next one. Every big task or long-term goal
may be divided into steps in progression. Instead of telling
yourself you'll never make a term grade of A in biology
because it seems so hard and far off, make plans to allow
enough time to study for your next quiz, and then put
your mind on that one step.

As you work yourself through what may be quite a
long pull, you occasionally (although not too often) stop
and take a look at how you are doing. How much progress
have you made? Does the goal seem any closer? Frequently
you will be pleasantly surprised at how well your sustained
effort is paying off. You may discover that you haven't lost
your temper in two weeks in spite of some temper-losing
temptations. You may realize that your mother is not
"bugging" you nearly as much as she did just a few weeks
ago.

On the other hand, your discoveries on progress may
be discouraging. But don't panic; ask yourself, "Why?"
Did you really not put forth the discipline and effort required? Was your effort not well directed? Do you need
more information or instruction? It is likely you can make
the necessary corrections to "do better" next time. All
persons experience false starts, and meet setbacks in
achievement, so you have lots of company, and having
found the trouble you can start again.

8. LOSING INTEREST IN A GOAL

After working toward a goal for some time you may discover that you are not making progress because you have lost interest in the goal; it no longer seems desirable. Or you may recognize that, contrary to what you thought at first, the goal is either beyond your capacity or has turned out to be too costly. In either case, after careful evaluation, you may decide to alter the goal. Suppose you find that a straight-A record requires a skill with words (high-level ability in reading and writing) that you do not now have. Therefore it would be more reasonable to aim for a B in those courses requiring such skill. Thus you scale down your goal; and you do it without embarrassment because anyone can misjudge the requirements of a goal as well as his own abilities. It is quite possible in most situations to take steps to increase your skill with words if you want to, and to aim for an A in a later semester. Changing or dropping a goal in midstream for good reasons is a mark of flexibility and good sense, not a sign of failure.

One caution, however: If you find yourself changing or dropping goals very frequently, something is wrong. Try to find out what it is. Perhaps you are not choosing goals with enough forethought; perhaps you are not seeing yourself with enough clarity; perhaps you are not yet sure what you want to become. Or, perhaps you are not exercising enough self-discipline.

Learning to manage goals in life wisely takes many years of experience, but the achievement helps to bring a bright future nearer.

SUCCESS AND FAILURE

The achievement or nonachievement of goals is tied up with success and failure in life. Most people want success and fear failure. The lives of most people include many experiences of both kinds. Let's see what success and failure mean. Understanding each one will help us to handle them.

Put very simply, success is the achievement of a goal that has been chosen and that has called forth effort. A person usually feels he is successful if he attains that which he wants—his goals. That is his own idea of whether or not he is successful. Other people looking at his attainments may have different views of his success. For example, Martin is a student who because of special abilities and skills makes high grades in his school subjects. Both his parents and his teachers look upon him as a "successful" student. But Martin does not see his situation in that way because his own goal in school is to be accepted and able to participate in some of the extracurricular activities such as the social clubs and the dramatic society. That goal he has not achieved, and therefore he sees himself as failing in what he wanted most in school. In other words, Martin does not give the same weight to his achievements in school subjects as some others do; this "success" does not satisfy him. It seems to be true that the success which really gives satisfaction to a person is the achievement of goals that he himself cherishes, rather than those which other people think he should want.

1. SUCCESS AND APPROVAL

The opinions of other people, however, often have a marked influence on the goals we consider important. In Martin's case, perhaps the other students do not see him as "successful," and this is why he himself feels his A's do not count for much. In that case, Martin is not really choosing for himself; he is accepting goals that he believes other students consider important. That fact may contribute to his sense of failure.

If we deliberately allow other people to set important goals for us, we often are not able to achieve the goals. We may fail in this achievement because we ourselves do not really believe in the goals. What we really want, in a situation of this kind, is the acceptance or approval of these other people. That is our real goal; and our feeling of having received this approval makes us feel "successful." Even when this kind of "success" is achieved, a person may feel that something is amiss down below the surface of things. Perhaps this feeling is caused by a half-formed recognition that he is not himself, but rather a picture of himself held by other people. If we are able to be clear-eyed about ourselves and our goals, to see what our real aims are, not just what they look like on the surface, we increase our capacity to shape the future, to become what we know we want to become, and thus at the same time we increase the chances of success.

Success, then, is the achievement of those goals that we have personally selected as our own and that we have worked at achieving. For the Christian, there is another dimension. Are those personally-selected goals in harmony with what he believes to be God's purposes? If so, their achievement will be his success, whether or not other people recognize it. For example, the white high school student who believes all persons are important to God, will really accept as a friend and fellow-student a Negro student in a newly integrated school. The white student believes this goal of living with others in respect and concern is appropriate for him. It is response to God's love for him. Other white students may find ways to punish him for living in accordance with a goal different from theirs; the Negro student may not appreciate his friendship. On the other hand, his attitude may stimulate similar attitudes among other white students; thus the Negro student may be received cordially and respond by being a fine member of the student body.

We would have to consider many things in this situation to decide whether or not the white student had been "successful" or had achieved his goal to live as a Christian in everyday experiences. The achievement of any significant goal is never an unqualified, or absolute, success. In all complex experiences of achievement there are likely to be elements of both failure and success. In many cases, it may not be appropriate to ask whether or not success was attained. God does not ask us to be "successful" in this sense; rather he asks us to be faithful in working toward goals in harmony with his purpose.

That is not to say that failure does not matter. But failure for the Christian comes in being unfaithful to our commitment to God, selecting unsuitable goals, or not putting forth an honest effort in working toward our goals. In the case of the white student in the paragraph above, he would have "failed" if he had ignored the situation of the new Negro student or if he had resented his presence.

The painful experience of failure is a part of the life of every person. In one sense, if we were never to fail, we might not be able to appreciate success. Many people think that we learn more, and hence add to our understandings and increase our capacities, when we fail than when we succeed. In order to learn through failure, however, we must find out where and why we went wrong, determine to make the necessary changes, and then try again. Some people never enter into this process of self-correction. They tend to put the blame for their failures on other people, and feel sorry for themselves. With this attitude they will probably keep on failing and feeling more and more abused and unhappy. It's both healthier and happier to admit whatever mistakes we make and set about doing what we can to make the next try a success.

2. SUCCESS AND YOUR RESPONSE

Let us look at one more factor in our consideration of success and failure in the achievement of goals.

John plays a skillful game of tennis after many years of working at it and enjoying the play. He decides to enter the community tennis tournament and his goal is to be the final winner. He plays hard and well, and he does win. His success is assured. His picture appears in the newspaper;

the sports reporter writes a glowing story of his skill and prowess. He is invited to a service club luncheon as a guest speaker, where total strangers tell him how remarkable he is. He begins to realize that he is a celebrity in the community; small boys look at him admiringly; even the girls his own age seem a little more friendly.

John is face to face with one of the major hazards of "success." How is he to respond to all this attention and admiration? Persons who observe and analyze human behavior say that "success" is much harder to handle in a mature and healthy way than "failure." This is so because when a person makes a public success in a field (such as sports) that people admire, they behave toward him in exaggerated ways. Often this is in ways that have nothing to do with the real achievement. If John has his feet on the ground and if he honestly understands what has happened, he will probably have some such response as this which he may put in the speech to the service club: It is nice for me that I won, but there is nothing remarkable about me; anyone who likes tennis enough to work hard to develop skill at it could have won; several other persons in the tournament might well have been the winner; the fact is, I could not have even played in this tournament had it not been for the help which I have had from many persons who have played against me through the years and made it possible for me to develop the necessary skills; tennis is a great game that brings much enjoyment to players; it is also a game that persons can enjoy almost all their lives; maybe our community should make it possible for more of our boys and girls to have the enjoyment of playing a good game of tennis.

On the other hand, it would have been easy for John to deceive himself, to believe the people who told him that he was "remarkable" and a hero in the community, to get pleasure out of taking all the credit for his achievement, to think only of himself, and to make much of the public acclaim. It is the temptation to yield to this kind of self-deception that makes handling success so hard.

But what about failure? Suppose John had not won. In that case he would have been what the public calls an "also-ran." John would naturally feel disappointed, perhaps sharply so. If, however, he and the other players put forth their best effort, he has the satisfaction of having engaged in a good game with all the enjoyment that comes from exercising a high-level skill. So his disappointment passes away rather quickly. He may have made a distinct gain by learning some things about tournament play that will improve his game. So John may conclude there is nothing very disturbing about this kind of "failure." But suppose John's disappointment continues and he feels envious of the public attention accorded the winner. Then he should take a second look at himself. What was his real goal? Winning the tournament or getting to be a "hero" in town? Perhaps his unconscious goal had been the latter.

We can remember some sober teachings of Jesus about any goal in life that would deliberately put us "above" other people. Here is one occasion in which Jesus talked with his disciples about such a goal:

Then the mother of the sons of Zebedee came up to him, with her sons, and kneeling before him she asked him for something. And he said to her, "What do you want?" She said to him, "Command that these two sons of mine may sit, one at your right hand and one at your left, in your kingdom." But Jesus answered, "You do not know what you are asking. Are you able to drink the cup that I am to drink?" They said to him, "We are able." He said to them, "You will drink my cup, but to sit at my right hand and at my left is not mine to grant, but it is for those for whom it has been prepared by my Father." And when the ten heard it, they were indignant at the two brothers. But Jesus called them to him and said, "You know that the rulers of the Gentiles lord it over them, and their great men exercise authority over them. It shall not be so among you; but whoever would be great among you must be your servant, and whoever would be first among you must be your slave; even as the Son of man came not to be served but to serve, and to give his life as a ransom for many."

—MATT. 20:20–28

3. SUCCESS AND WHAT YOU BECOME

Perhaps we can conclude that while success and failure are realities in the achievement of sought-after goals, they are not the most important reality. More important than success is the choosing of the goal itself, because it will influence what we will become. And most important of all in thinking about and planning for the future, is learning more about God's purposes for us and responding in faith. On that firm basis we may have a hand in shaping our destiny and in living strong and significant lives, not because of the success we achieve but because of what we *are*—persons who know we have worth in the eternal scheme of things, and that what we are and what we do are important to ourselves, to others around us, to the human family, to God.

5.

WHAT WILL MY LIFE BE LIKE?

AT first it seems rather silly to ask the question, "What will my life be like?" Even when dreaming of what you will become as a person, you know you cannot see into the future clearly enough to describe what will happen to you. It is true: None of us is able to predict the circumstances of his future life. And yet it is equally true that some choices are open to you. You not only may set goals but you may also decide the general outlines of what your life will be like.

This is so because what your life is does not depend entirely upon the things that happen to you. Your real life—that which brings you satisfaction—is built from what you make of what happens to you, the meaning it has for you. Your view of the external conditions of your life, what you do about events and occasions, your response to people and to happenings—these matters are most important in making up your life, and they are largely in your own hands. In other words, though many events and happenings are beyond your control, what your life will be like is to a significant degree up to you. Except for the radically handicapped or oppressed, every person has some capacity to build a life that to him has meaning and satisfaction, and that can contribute something to the lives of other persons.

We have this power and capacity because of who we are: children of God, created in his image, and possessing many endowments in varying degrees. These endowments characterize us as persons, and may be thought of as powers of body, mind, and spirit, each related to the others and functioning together in "personality." Herein lies our true self-confidence. Because of these gifts with which human beings have been endowed, every young person may feel confident of himself. As we have seen, this does not mean that every person can do everything he wants to do, nor does it mean that all people have equal endowments. But generally a person can do a great many things out of which he may build a satisfying life. Every person has much to learn about the way to overcome his limitations and the way to develop and use his gifts; also he requires much practice in making judgments in carrying out plans. The important point, however, is that no one should feel despairing because of lack of confidence in himself as a *person*. Especially no young person.

Sometimes we observe what we think is self-confidence

in others—bragging talk, aggressive behavior, the ability to manipulate others and "get what they want"—and because we are not willing or able to act in this way we think we do not have self-confidence. This kind of behavior, how-ever, is often a cover-up for *lack* of self-confidence. The person with genuine confidence in himself is willing to learn about himself and the world, to take initiative, to make decisions, to instigate both short and long-term plans, to engage in a course of action, to evaluate and learn from the results of a course of action. This evidence of self-confidence is related to the selection and pursuit of personal goals as described in the previous chapter.

The person who exercises his capacities in this way is the one who is not defeated by disadvantageous circum-stances; he is able to respond with courage and resourceful-ness to the disappointing and hurtful events in life which come to everyone. He is not saved from all suffering and unhappiness. These come to all men. But he has ways of doing something positive about what happens. "Doing something" is not always overt action; it may be appro-priating a "saving" attitude—that is, an attitude which rescues a person from excessive discouragement, thus mov-ing the situation away from hopelessness.

YOUR STYLE OF LIFE

The way you want your life to be may be called its "style." While you are still young enough to be a part of your parents' home, you can begin to experiment, to try out various plans in order to discover what style suits you best. Then when you make your own home (whether or not you are married), you are in position to go farther in building your own style. When two persons marry, they should consider whether they both have or want a reasonably similar style of life. It is not necessary that they agree in every respect, but the life they build together should hold some of the same basic satisfactions for each partner.

Geneva sat alone in the drug store, and delayed going home from school because she was afraid. She knew she could not face the scene with her parents when she told them she was failing her math course. The feeling of being trapped was overwhelming. She saw herself as the stupid member of the family, not like her sister Jane who always had good grades in high school, even in math. Geneva felt she was failing in everything—not only in school work but also in being socially popular. As her despair deepened she told herself, "I'm no good; life's terrible; I wish I were out of it."

Apparently Geneva thinks she is "no good" because she compares herself with Jane; she seems to think she should be "another Jane" instead of herself, Geneva. It may be that Geneva's parents, and even Jane, have encouraged this view. By what they say or by their attitude they may have shown they wanted Geneva to be like Jane. So here is Geneva in tears because she is not Jane.

Put in this way Geneva's problem does not look so "horrible." If she could see herself as Geneva, not Jane, she could find that far from being "no good," she has capacities and abilities which she might properly regard as "good." They would likely be different from Jane's, and possibly her activities and relationships at school would not be those of her sister. Her goals and achievements would be different, but no less satisfying and worthful.

If Geneva can begin to think about herself in this way, she is learning about herself and is taking a big step forward in being herself, instead of an unsuccessful copy of Jane. In order to think along these lines, however, Geneva must lay hold on those two wonderful gifts to men that go together —freedom and responsibility. No matter who may have influenced her in her attempt to copy Jane, Geneva herself must take steps to change this attitude. It is no use just to blame someone else and feel miserable and powerless.

An attempt to change an attitude is being responsible— acknowledging that your attitudes and behavior are your own, and that you can not lay either all the blame or all the credit on other people. Accepting this responsibility goes along with being free to exercise it, that is, to learn and change. Geneva need not feel trapped; she is in trouble but she can work at getting out of trouble. Possibly in her situation she should reconsider her entire school program in light of what she has learned about herself. She may get help from adults in her school or church, or others in whom she has trust. When she has recognized the confidence that is really hers, she may be able to help her parents understand that she is Geneva, a distinctive person in her own right, and that she will never be like Jane. Perhaps some counselor can help her in changing her parents' expectations. Thus Geneva is beginning to build her own style of life, which she can do because she is learning about herself and taking some responsibility for being herself.

As you think about your own style of life—what life will be like for you—consider these suggestions.

1. A "Coping" Style of Life

Willingness to use your freedom in taking responsibility for significant parts of your life is what some psychologists call a "coping" style of life. To cope with something is to do something about it that is constructive and healthful. You hear people say, "I can't cope with this. Someone will have to do it for me." In some instances this is accurate. Some situations and types of responsibility are beyond the capacity of some persons to handle or "cope with." If, however, these persons seek legitimate help, as Geneva would be doing in getting counsel from appropriate adults, this act is one way of "coping."

Some persons, on the other hand, give up, fail to put any energy into the situation, and become "dependent" persons, relying on other people to arrange things for them, and to "carry" them through life. This attitude of "dependency" is a "non-coping" style of life and means that the person has rejected the twin gifts of freedom and responsibility. When the person's dependency becomes severe he may have to be hospitalized for professional treatment. Most persons, however, can learn to develop a coping style of life, and so enjoy the satisfactions of full participation in life through decision-making and responsible action.

The coping style of life that guards against attitudes and behavior of "dependency" does not mean that any person is absolutely "independent." As we have already seen, all persons must depend upon other people for help and service all their lives. Therefore our "independence" and our self-reliance are limited. Especially for young people, it is important to be ready to seek legitimate help when it is appropriate to do so. We can also learn to accept this kind of help without feeling a lack of confidence in ourselves. In Geneva's case, seeking the advice of the school counselors in reviewing and perhaps rearranging her school program is to enlist legitimate help. On the other hand, Geneva might give in to her feelings, accept her "failure" as inevitable, and then expect to get special sympathy or even favors from teachers and friends because of incapacity—a kind of "help" which she feels will make her situation more endurable. Such "help" is not legitimate because it increases her dependency, her lack of self-confidence and personhood, and so of her unhappiness.

Because none of us is one-hundred per cent independent, each of us must be willing to extend legitimate help to other persons. In Geneva's case again, it may be that Jane is one who could be especially helpful to her sister by encouraging Geneva's changed attitude, by taking special notice of Geneva's achievements, by not displaying her own accomplishments, even by soliciting Geneva's help when she genuinely needs it. If Jane can be helpful in this way she will have rendered a fine service to Geneva. Also a healthy interdependence may grow between the two sisters. "Interdependence" describes the desired relationship among free and responsible human beings, each recognizing that he needs the other.

2. A Broad and Inclusive Style of Life

A popular quotation some years ago stated that "The world is so full of a number of things, I'm sure we should all be as happy as kings." It fell into disfavor because it is too "rosy"; this view of the world does not take into account those things that clearly do not make us happy, and also because the fact is that kings are no more likely to be happy than are other people. Even so, "the world is so full of a number of things" is a suitable way to begin comment on another characteristic of a style of life.

In Chapter Three we explored the opportunities and challenges of life. Building on what was said there, we may discover ways in which such challenges and opportunities may help us develop a life style.

A Variety of Activities

An important way is deliberately to work toward a style of life that includes a broad range of activities and many different kinds of people. The two key words in that sentence are "range" and "different."

A range of activities does not necessarily imply a large number of activities or a lot of busyness. Range means variety and scope. It implies not doing the same thing all the time, not restricting your interest to just a few items. For instance, if you find yourself playing the same games, listening to the same music, pursuing the same hobby, always doing the same thing in your free time—your style of life may be too narrow. It also may be dull and unexciting because there is not enough of the unknown, not enough chance for adventure or surprise.

If your record collection tends to center on the music of Bach and Mozart, trying listening to some first-class jazz; if it is built around the latest pop tunes, trying listening to both Bach and jazz, which have a lot in common. If your game is baseball, try adding a table game like checkers, or even chess. If you spend a lot of time with electronic gadgets, try painting a picture. If your summer Saturdays are spent with a power boat, experiment with paddling a canoe. If you have been on the school's debating team, try out for the dramatic society, or, for a real change, the star-gazing club. Just because your taste runs to "french fries," don't turn down mother's artichoke casserole. Once in a while try something you think you won't like. It may be going to a performance of ballet or to a football game, or reading Melville's *Moby Dick* or the Bible, or visiting a home for the aged in your community, or even the zoo.

Especially while you are young, you should try out many kinds of interests and activities, because in this way you discover much about yourself—what you can do, what gives you satisfaction, what holds possibilities for your future, what captures your imagination. You may not enjoy all the interests you experiment with, but they will open up the possibility of new and enriching experiences. Your style of life takes on additional verve and vigor; you may develop a variety of interests and skills.

This kind of experimentation requires initiative, planning, and selectivity. Some new things may just happen to present themselves, but most of them must be sought out. You may get in touch with new interests by listening to other people tell about their activities, by reading a book recommended by one of your teachers or a friend or relative, by keeping up with newspapers and magazines to see what is happening and what people are doing in your home town and in the wide world.

To experiment with a new interest, you must make plans for how and when to begin. Often "when" is the hardest part because it requires time and maybe scheduling. Unless we are watchful about what happens to our time, we find that each twenty-four hours is taken up with trivial and casual items which don't really interest us, or we find time on our hands to fill with nothing planned that we like doing. A good start is to look ahead to next week for a specific time for that trip to the music store, or for the tennis game, the lesson in checkers, or playing in the combo, or whatever will open up a new interest.

Again, a caution may be helpful. Being selective, taking pains to choose carefully, is necessary in building an inclusive style of life. To be inclusive is not "trying everything." Some kinds of interests are not worth the time they take. Some you know in advance may be harmful to yourself or others. So look ahead, consider the consequences, the value, the requirements, in planning to expand your interests. Don't try too many things at once. If you hop from one interest to the next without giving any one enough time and attention for a real try-out, you do not discover much about any of them.

The Place of People

Probably more important than a range of activities in an inclusive style of life are different kinds of people. All persons tend to feel more comfortable and congenial with persons they think are like them. This point was explored in Chapter Two. Following up what was said there, you can see the value to your life of associations and friendships with persons different from yourself in nationality, in age, in interests, in skills, in race, in social background. These experiences enlarge your point of view, increase your understanding of people and the world, deepen your satisfactions in living. Persons who restrict their associations to a small sphere, rarely coming in contact with anyone outside their immediate circles, are very likely to be ignorant about large areas of life and narrow-minded on social and intellectual issues. A better style of life will provide for moving beyond your immediate circle of associates, or for bringing different kinds of people into your circle.

If you live in a middle-size or large city and attend a large high school, you may find ready-made opportunities for breaking open your circle. Even so, you may have to take the initiative. Extend an invitation to some person you know in the school who lives in a section of the city different from yours, or who goes to a different church, or who comes from a national background different from yours, or whose school activities are different. The invitation may be for a trip to the local museum, to play a game, to listen to records, to go swimming. Such an invitation will be made on the basis that you have a real interest in getting to know the other person, not that you are making an "experiment." You "experiment" with activities but not with persons. To do the latter is to treat a person as a thing to be used in your behalf, and not to relate to him as another human being and a child of God.

If you live in a small town or a rural section or a restricted suburb, you may have fewer opportunities for relationships with many kinds of people. Sometimes families plan trips that will enlarge their acquaintance with and their understanding of a wider variety of persons. If you live in a town, a visit to a relative who lives in a metropolitan center may provide interesting opportunities. A reverse visit is also a possibility. David, who lived in a very large city, spent two weeks with his uncle who worked with 4-H clubs. He had many interesting times with young people on farms as he accompanied his uncle on his trips around the county.

To know and appreciate different kinds of people will not necessarily result in your becoming "best" or even close friends with them, although it may. The essential point is to recognize and accept persons as worthful human beings when they are "different" or even "strange." In order to maintain this attitude, which is our obligation because we are all children of God, our style of life must include some ways of getting to know a wide variety of people. And as we have seen, this inclusive life-style requires initiative and planning.

THE USES OF MONEY

When you dream about what your life will be like, many times you wonder, "What will I have?" Will you have the kinds of possessions you think important or even essential? Sometimes the things a person wants become the focus of his dreams and plans. An instance is the case of Mike in the previous chapter. There we considered the getting of money as a goal in life. Here we are exploring the ways in which we deal with money in developing a style of life.

One of the features of our society is that it is a money-economy. Our economic arrangements rest on the use and manipulation of money. All persons are consumers of goods and services for which they or persons on their behalf pay money. Many persons produce these goods and services for which usually they receive money. This flow of money throughout the complicated buying-and-selling system keeps the economy alive and growing. When a money economy runs down, or worse, when it comes to a standstill, economic "depression" results with wide-scale suffering and deprivation. There is some suffering and deprivation even when a money-economy is running well, as we can see today in the rural slums and in large sections of city life in our country. (Remember Tony in the previous chapter.) In our society these are not considered "normal." But in an economic "depression," deprivation is much more widespread, and much of it is very severe. We can see, therefore, that money is important in our society. The way any individual regards money and uses it is even more important. And so the place of money in your style of life requires consideration.

To get some perspective, let's first consider what money is. In itself money has no value. That is true of large sums in a bank and of the small change in your pocket. As long as it stays in your pocket, it is good only for a jingle. Money becomes valuable when it is used, when you take it out of your pocket and spend it for something —a telephone call, a book, a ticket to a movie, an ice-cream cone for your little sister, a contribution to the school band uniforms, or to the church library fund.

Money may also be spent in a way to produce more money. This would happen on a small scale if you took the money from your pocket and deposited it in a savings account in a bank. It is equally true that money accumulated in a bank has no value until it is used, or spent. That is why banks lend money, for then it is being used. The bank uses your money in a savings account in this way. And so your money earns more money to be used for a variety of purposes and needs of people.

This fact about money shows that it is never an end, only a means to achieve an end. Now, the ends for which money is used are determined by principles and values. This applies to the way you spend the coins in your pocket as well as to the way a bank lends money. And here is the heart of the question. It is the way you use, or spend, what money you have, whether in large or small amounts, that is significant. An important part of your style of life is the use you make of money, and the attitude you have toward money and the things which money will buy.

At the present stage in your life, you may or may not have much money that is yours to spend as you wish. But however much it is, you have the responsibility of deciding how to use it, and of developing the appropriate place of money in your life style. Here are a number of questions to consider in your use of money.

Just what satisfaction will any particular expenditure provide? Will it provide something I need? Something I will enjoy? Or only something I want right now? Sometimes we think we want things that we neither need nor that will bring us much satisfaction. Often we think we want things just because other people have them. It is not smart to buy things others have (a particular piece of clothing, or small radio, or charm bracelet, or a popular book, or a tool, or pair of skates) without asking what value these things will have for *me*.

What part of my money shall I spend for possessions and what part for experiences? Generally possessions refer to things you have and use like clothes, and experiences refer to things you do, like going to a movie. Some things fall in both classes; for example, riding your bicycle, reading your book, listening to your record player. Spending money for taking a trip, going to camp, joining a club, attending sports events, concerts, plays, taking lessons in music or golf is money spent for experiences.

Most persons find they want to include both possessions and experiences in their spending. In many cases, experiences such as the ones cited require a larger outlay of money than some possessions. Most persons must plan in advance and deliberately not spend money on unimportant things if they are to have the kinds of experiences they want. Persons differ in the value they place on possessions as against experiences. Some people think that an interesting and enjoyable experience is more lasting in value than most kinds of possessions. Other people get more pleasure out of having possessions. Your point of view on this question will influence what your life will be like.

Another important question is: What part of my spending will be for myself and what part for other people? When we explored opportunities for service in Chapter Three, we were aware that in some situations our best form of service is providing money to meet needs of other people. These people may be in our private world (friends and family) or in our public world (the local community or some community far away). If a person's style of life does not include using money on behalf of other people, including those who need his service but whom he can never see and know face to face, he will not develop imagination and concern. This will detract from his style of life. The self-centered and self-indulgent person is usually an unhappy and unsatisfied person because it is part of being human that we cannot live fully and abundantly apart from interest in and concern for other people.

When thinking about spending money it is a good idea to ask: Why do I want to do this? This question will prod us to look at our motivations before spending. Sometimes we are surprised at what we find. Maybe we are spending money in the expectation that people will be impressed or look up to us (prestige, status), or possibly even love us. Many people have learned from unhappy experience that using money in this way is futile. This is really spending money to show off, or to use a big word, for ostentation. Perhaps certain of our acquaintances will take notice, and we will bask in the attention of the moment. But the most we can really get for our money spent in this way is envy from other people. And that is a sword with two edges, because persons tend to turn against the people they envy. The fact is that money cannot buy admiration, esteem, and love. Rather it works the other way: Many times we spend money out of our own admiration and love of others. They may or may not love and admire us.

The motivation for spending money is related to the basic principles and values in living, which we have considered and which grow out of who we are, what we are here for, what we want to become. Although money is important, it is never as important as people. The same is true of the possessions money buys. This is recognized in the public economy where we have protective laws against the abuse of persons to increase profits.

In our private uses of money we recognize that sometimes money is used carelessly to degrade people, so that they feel less than human. If a young person in a group spends lots of money when the others have much less to spend, he is degrading his friends. They will feel separated from him and they may conclude that he is deliberately insulting their dignity as persons. The point is not that this person had more money to spend than his friends but that he used it in a way to hurt them. Even if he spends the money "for" his friends by always paying for the treats, they will still be hurt, although they may accept.

On the other hand, sometimes persons with very little money exploit or abuse persons with more money by playing on their sympathies to get things from them. Usually such persons are motivated by envy or a sense of injustice. In short, both the "haves" and the "have nots" in society may be tempted to use money to hurt other persons.

A safeguard against this kind of hurtful experience is to think about the "human values" involved in any expenditure: What will the consequences be to persons? Another way is to emphasize and to derive our satisfactions from our enjoyment of the people themselves, not from the possessions or the money, if any, involved in our friendship with them.

All along we have been thinking of the money you have to spend over and beyond that which goes for life's necessities. Parents usually provide young people with the necessities of living out of the family budget. You may already be aware of the money your family must spend for housing, the family car, basic clothing, church, community organizations, food, medicine, doctors' services, education, and the like. If it is the custom in your family, you may help to decide on some of these expenditures. Perhaps you contribute to the family budget out of earnings from part-time work on Saturdays or on a paper route or through baby sitting. If so, you may have already learned some of the difficulties and some of the satisfactions in the support of a family, and to understand the responsibility of the family wage-earner(s). You may find this experience valuable in planning the uses of money in your future style of life.

LIVING WITH CHANGE

When you think about the style of your future life, there is one thing you can count on: The world will have changed in many important ways from the world you live in at present. People who have the skill to make forecasts of this kind tell us that in the latter half of the twentieth century people will move around even more than they do now; the situation respecting jobs and occupations will radically change; all areas are likely to be more crowded with people living and working more closely together; opportunities for adding richness and enjoyment to life will increase; the business of running the institutions of society will be vastly more complicated; the need for good judgment, informed opinion, and moral insight and conviction will be much more urgent.

Some of the reasons for these changes to come lie in the rapid advance in technology (more and better machines to help perform the world's work), the availability of more and more knowledge, the increased population, the expansion of physical power.

In this future all persons will be expected to live with change, to be flexible and sensitive to the movements that may rapidly alter the circumstances of their lives. Much of this change will make possible better lives for more people. At the same time, persons must be prepared to meet these several revolutions with intelligence, accurate information, and sound interpretation. But even more, people must know how to evaluate the currents of change so as to make ethical decisions about them. They must decide which changes do and which do not support human betterment in line with God's purposes for his children, so far as human beings can understand them.

Actually the world is opening up before you, the young generation, in ways undreamed of in the past. No adult can precisely describe this future world of yours. No adult can tell you exactly how to respond in it. Things will be different, but it will be your world in which you may develop your own strong and flexible style of life.

A CHRISTIAN VIEW OF A STYLE OF LIFE

So far in this chapter we have explored ways of developing a style of life by reviewing and illustrating concrete situations and specific questions. There are, however, some generalizations that are appropriate to all such practical matters. These generalizations express a coming together of meaning, and are valuable to a person each day because they help him answer new questions and cope with new situations as they arise. For those who think of themselves as children of God, these meanings gather around and are expressed in two words from the Christian vocabulary.

1. STEWARDSHIP

In the Christian vocabulary, the word for the way money and possessions are regarded is "stewardship." The "steward" is one who uses something in the name of or on behalf of another. Early in this book we noted the belief of Christians that God is the Creator of all that is. Therefore God is the ultimate, or final, owner of all that is—the entire natural world and all its resources, including possessions and money. This belief in God's ownership means that what we "own" is not, in the final sense, ours but God's. Therefore, Christians believe that all persons are entrusted with these things by God in order to use them in his name and in harmony with his purposes. We are "stewards" of God's world. Our "stewardship" extends very widely and includes the management of time, energy, talents, natural resources, the arrangements for a healthy economy, as well as the ways of spending money in our personal style of life. It is clear from Jesus' teaching that God wants us to use all the world's resources, public and private, responsibly, and to further his purposes for all people.

When we willingly perform services for other people, whether or not any money is involved, we are acting in God's name and out of love for him and his people. When we spend our personal money, or when older people vote on the uses of public taxes, all of us are fulfilling our stewardship, that is, we make such decisions in light of our belief that God has entrusted us to use what we have in ways that will help ourselves and other people to live out his purposes for a good life.

As we have seen, the Christian concept of stewardship applies not only to money; but to all we have—special gifts, resources of personality. The same questions we ask about the use of money are appropriate as we consider using other resources at our disposal. Our attitude toward and our use of time and talents, for instance, come under the influence of our role as God's stewards. Therefore we answer many questions about "What will my life be like?" by considering the opportunities and obligations of Christian stewardship.

2. VOCATION

Another word in the Christian vocabulary that has important meaning for developing a style of life is "vocation." In the general vocabulary, "vocation" refers to "job," "occupation," or "livelihood." In the Christian vocabulary, "occupation" is only one of the meanings of "vocation." Its meaning includes also the basic values and loyalties in a person's life in whatever occupation he earns a living. These values and loyalties shape and direct everything a person does, and the whole trend of his life. This fact was explored in detail under "What Am I Here For?" and "What Will I Become?" Accordingly we speak of the "vocation of the Christian" when we mean the total outlook and life style of the Christian—that is, the life to which he has been "called" by God. (The English "vocation" comes from the Latin "vocare" which means "to call".) This is true whether he be a doctor or a lumberjack or a homemaker or a lawyer or a professional athlete or teacher or a mechanic or a minister or a farmer. As he does his job, he is called also to follow his vocation as a child of God.

Again we affirm that we are God's children by our response to his work in creation. We are in the world—the world of human life and endeavor as well as the world of nature—to be his children and to live out our vocation as Christians. The style of life of the person who is committed to God in faith and love will reflect both his sense of stewardship and his vocation as a Christian.

6.

WHERE DO
I FIT IN?

YOU know from your own experience as well as from
other sources that persons cannot be complete selves
apart from other persons. As has been said in previous
chapters of this book, not only are we dependent on one
another for our survival on this planet, but most people are
unhappy and unsatisfied if they do not have frequent and
rather prolonged association with other people. This need
of people gives rise to human societies, cultures, and civilizations. In the lives of individuals this need stimulates the
formation of a great variety of groups.

THE GROUPS IN YOUR LIFE

Think of the groups you belong to. First, of course, is your
family, which is often spoken of as the basic unit in society.

Every infant is born into some kind of family, if not the usual two-parent-brother-and-sister family, then one or more persons who substitute for the usual type of family. A family group remains the primary one for most persons almost all their lives, because when a young person leaves his parents' home, he usually establishes his own family within a few years, or perhaps immediately. Some kind of family group persists for most people, although the strength of the ties among the family members will vary widely.

You may belong to one or more neighborhood groups made up of the young people living near to you with whom you associate informally in your free time more or less regularly. Add to the list your school groups, not only classes but also social clubs and groups that are interested in various activities, such as the school paper, the football team, the band, the literary society. You may belong also to some hobby, sport, or skill group not affiliated with the school.

As you grow older, the number of groups you belong to will likely increase. An important one will probably be a work group. For most boys and men and for many girls and women some kind of work group will continue for many years of life. Related are such groups as luncheon clubs and service clubs.

To the on-going type of group may be added such special groups as political organizations and those interested in aspects of community life—school, welfare, taxes. The purposes, activities, and the duration of these groups will be different from one another, but the total "group experiences" of any person are likely to add up to a large part of his life.

MY PLACE IN "COMMUNITY"

It seems, therefore, that one answer to "Where Do I Fit In?" is that you fit into groups of many kinds. Or to say it another way, you fit into "community." The word "community" has much meaning for human life. Basically it means an association of persons with one or more common elements. The word "common" comes from the same root as "community." This common element may be merely the fact that the people live in the same town and thereby form a unit of society. When we speak of "the local community" we are using the word in this sense. But associations of persons may have other elements in common—shared purposes, loyalty, and skills (the football team); shared interest (the garden club, the bike club, the square dance group); a shared cause to be supported and propogated (the Young Democrats or Republicans). These common elements pull people together and lay the base for a "community."

"Community" has a further meaning. Not only does the word designate a group of people, it also points to and implies the quality of the group-life among the people. The kind of life the people in a group have together may or may not be characterized by "community." To belong to a group is not necessarily to be in "community" with the members of the group. A group may be just a collection of individuals without any real feeling of interest in or concern for one another. So long as they remain only a collection, the group will not be very meaningful to the members nor will it accomplish much as a group. It seems that persons in groups find meaning and satisfaction only when the group attains the quality of "community." Without it few groups survive. Thus, it seems that persons fit into groups best when they achieve "community"; and that persons may fit into any situation where there is "community."

Because our experiences in groups are so many and so persistent, we should consider some of the ways by which a group achieves "community," and the significance for all persons of living in "community."

DISCIPLINES OF GROUP LIFE

The quality of the life of any group depends upon what the members make of it. The persons who participate in any group are responsible for its life. They are the ones who are able to make of the group a community by the attitudes they sustain, the understandings they hold, and the behavior they engage in. All the concepts, principles, and values discussed in previous chapters are pertinent to our participation in any group from a basic and intimate one, like the family, to one that is short-term and designed for one limited purpose, like the committee to plan an assembly program at school.

Group life, however, calls on persons to accept special disciplines that are based on these concepts, principles, and values. "Discipline" in this sense means a rule of conduct, or a way of behaving, that a person accepts and agrees to follow. Let us explore some of these disciplines that are likely to foster the achievement of community. They will also suggest the reasons why living in community is so important and rewarding to every person.

1. UNDERTAKING RESPONSIBILITY

An important discipline, or way of behaving, in a group is to undertake responsibility. Most groups are formed to do something, that is, some kind of long- or short-term purpose. Even if the group's purpose is limited to discussion, it will not be a good group unless the members participate responsibly by arriving on time, and taking part in the deliberations. When a purpose requiring actual work is involved, each person must do his share or carry his part of the load. To belong to a group and to be unwilling to undertake responsibility for carrying out the group's purpose is to be a parasite, living on the labors of others. It is also a kind of "living outside" rather than "living inside" the group, even though you may be present when the group meets. The values of community come only to the persons who are willing to assume their share of the group's tasks.

This sharing in the work of a group does not mean that every person does the same thing. In some groups, such as a class, a family, a club, a committee, different persons take different roles. The parent's role is different from the child's, the teacher's role is different from the student's, although they perform many of the same tasks. Also, a chairman of a committee, or president of a club, sometimes has a special role that is not assumed by every member.

Furthermore, persons vary in their capacities and resources. Just as not every member of a football team plays the same position, not every member of other groups can assume the same kind of responsibility. The point is that each person should decide what he can do best to contribute to the over-all life of the group or the specific task undertaken and be willing to spend the necessary time and effort to do it well. Some individuals seem to like to be with the people but not to assume any responsibility for or in the group. Such a person never derives the deeper satisfactions of group life. In addition, his attitude is likely to be resented by the other people. Doing things together, especially those requiring skill and competence, is more fun and more rewarding than just inactive belonging to a group.

This attitude of assuming responsibility is especially significant in the family. It is clear to most people that parents must work in and for the family, but it is not always assumed that even a small child can take some responsibility and perform some kind of work. Older children naturally assume larger tasks. If you have learned in your family to take appropriate responsibility, you will find participation in other groups easier and more interesting.

2. A "CARING-FOR" ATTITUDE

Sometimes persons want to do their share of the work within a group but are too shy to volunteer, or are afraid they won't be able to meet the responsibility successfully. This situation leads to another discipline of group life— members should be willing to help one another. This caring-for one another is really the basis of healthy group life as well as the cement that holds the individuals of the group together in community.

Thus each member accepts the discipline that he will help the others to assume appropriate roles and undertake responsibility in ways suitable to them. This help may include furnishing resources such as transportation or equipment, acting as a teacher in skill practice (more experienced members of the Camera Club teach needed skills to the less experienced), encouraging others to take part in discussion or activity, and welcoming their contributions; using one's strength or tallness to help a frail member do a physical job.

On occasions a caring-for attitude may mean protecting a member of the group from ridicule or teasing, or taking his part when he is under attack. It is important to recognize that this helping type of behavior is not reserved for your special friends, or those with whom you feel especially congenial. Community among persons extends to all persons in the group, or it is not community. To be active in caring for those in the group you don't like, or disagree with, or feel hostile toward requires a deliberate effort, sometimes forcing yourself to say and do some-

thing you would rather not. This is one reason this behavior is called a discipline. Frequently, but not always,
such action forges a bond between you and another person
which each of you finds satisfying.

The other side is important, too. In such a group you
will likely receive the kind of help that enables you to
participate more actively, to learn more readily, to be accepted more fully, and therefore to be more accepting of
yourself and of others.

The specific behavior called for by this helping attitude
will vary according to the purpose and kind of group involved. In a group such as a family or certain types of
church groups the members sustain quite intimate relationships with one another; therefore the help given and received is often very personal or even private. A group
organized around an interest in a hobby or sport or community clean-up would probably not lend itself to intimate
relationships, but the opportunities for supporting and
helping one another are real. Often you can give needed
support to another person by listening to him and showing
an interest in his activities and his ideas and opinions. This
sort of support is closely akin to "concern" and "service"
as discussed in Chapter Three.

It may be that all members of a group will not undertake the discipline of helping one another; in fact, it is a
rare group in which all persons do. Even so, the true
human being—that is, one who is living up to his personhood under God—will accept this discipline in his group
life. Because persons are created for community, often

many of them will respond to the efforts of even one person to build community through a caring-for attitude. It is possible for such a one to transform the life of a group.

3. Some "Don'ts" for Group Life

We must also recognize some things that destroy community and that suggest some "don'ts" for group life.

One of these "don'ts" is excessive showing-off or continued bids for attention. Some persons have a real talent for being amusing or diverting before an audience, or for pressing their ideas and opinions so strongly that other people must listen. Either type of behavior is a bid for attention and a kind of showing off; it is also the kind of contribution that a group often needs and appreciates. It becomes a "don't" when it keeps other people from claiming their share of attention, and when it hampers rather than supports the group. You have probably been in a class or a club when one person took so much time being amusing that the purpose for the class or club meeting could not be carried out. You also know of persons who talk so much about their ideas that no one else has a chance to describe his ideas. Every member needs and has a right to claim his share of attention from other people, but not in such a way as to keep other people from their share.

Another "don't" has to do with domination. No one person or combination of persons should try to be allowed to dictate the decisions of a group, or dominate its affairs. When a group gives in to the wishes or opinions of one person all the time, the members have really become slaves, and have denied that they are free and responsible persons. When one person expects the group always to follow his lead, he is a dictator seeking to live above the others and thus not as a full human being. Community is achieved through the free interplay among responsible human beings.

One important helping role is to alert the group to attempts at domination—always doing what Susanne wants, or believing what Jack says. And vice versa, a good group member will be willing to accept the situation gracefully when the group does not follow his ideas or advice. Thus, a person with a strong tendency to dominate will restrain his impulses and learn to sit easily with the give-and-take of the group. This is but a negative way of saying that in community all persons share in and have responsibility for the life of the group.

4. WILLINGNESS TO BE YOURSELF

Another discipline of group life is the willingness and obligation to be yourself, both in and in spite of the group. We have spoken often of the individual's uniqueness. It is persons and not groups that are created by God as free and responsible human beings. Whenever we allow any group to take over large areas of our lives to the extent that we no longer feel free and able to make our own decisions, we are no longer individual persons. This sort of thing is likely to happen to young people in some social clubs or strong neighborhood groups. To be a free individual means that sometimes we must be ourselves in spite of the wishes of a group we cherish. On occasion we must say: This is not for me, or, I must do this in spite of what you think.

Of course, we will be influenced by the ideas and the behavior of the groups we live with. In this way we grow and learn. But to be influenced does not mean to be absorbed so that we no longer have minds of our own. Each decision is ours to make. If a group tries to be a true community it will encourage each person to be himself, and to stand over against the group when necessary. This is the reason that a true democracy living by the will of the majority always provides for the rights of a minority. It is the reason that when a decision of the Supreme Court is not unanimous, the minority opinion also is given publicity. When a group denies to each member the right to be himself and to express his own opinion it has become a herd of faceless robots—not a community of persons.

Sometimes a group will punish a member for differing with its customs or ways of thinking. Again, that is the mark of the herd. A herd may be and often is a strong force, but among persons it should be resisted all along the way because it destroys community and subverts human beings.

It is a good tactic in any group to affirm your individuality in the beginning and to support others in doing so. That often will prevent your becoming unduly entangled so that you can't get free as easily later on. On the other hand, if you find yourself continually standing over against a group, you may well ask yourself whether this attitude comes from your wish to be a real person, or your wish to get attention or to dominate. This temptation will even arise in groups that make no effort to suppress persons as individuals. To differ just for the sake of differing is to hinder community just as truly as is an attitude of uncritical conformity.

Sometimes the problem may be that this particular group is somehow inappropriate for you. You don't enjoy it or find interest in it. Or its activities seem to you foolish or harmful. We should not have the notion that every group is appropriate for each one of us.

In exploring what it means to stand against a group, we must make a clear distinction. To maintain your right to differ from the majority view in any group is not the same thing as to defy the person or persons in the group who represent appropriate authority. Teachers and principals, parents and policemen, are persons who speak for a constituted authority related to the general welfare and safety and involving several kinds of groups.

There have been times when it was necessary for the Christian to defy a recognized authority related to his group life. (Such as a Christian in Nazi Germany protecting a Jew, or a Christian in the United States protecting a child in a family from a brutal father or protecting a student of a minority group from school regulations unfair to him.) Here, however, we do not refer to that kind of action, which is in a different category and is related to another issue. For most of us most of the time respect for legitimate authority is a requirement of responsible personhood. In the case of Geneva in the previous chapter, she is not defying her parents' authority; she is trying to alter their view of what she is like, including her particular capacities and gifts.

The center of the meaning of this discipline in group life is that we must work for an equilibrium between the values of experiences in groups and the values of affirming oneself as a free and unique individual. When we can distinguish between these two sets of values, we can direct our efforts toward conserving both of them.

5. CLARIFYING THE PURPOSE OF A GROUP

One more discipline, which underlies the others, must be mentioned. In undertaking this discipline you, along with all other members, attempt to discover the purpose that moves the group to action and the values or ideals that its life supports. This discovery comes in answer to the questions: What are we doing in our life together? What guides our decisions and relationships with one another and with other groups? For example, what are we aiming for as the main purpose in this social club? To increase each member's opportunities for parties and other fun-things? To learn the niceties of social etiquette? To keep people out of this club? To extend opportunities for social activities more widely on the school campus?

To take another example. What values does this football team represent in the school? The value of winning games by whatever means we can? The value of rigorous team play? The value of personal glory to team members? The value of being part of a favored few? The value of bringing prestige to the school? The value of extending an interest in sports to more members of the student body?

A third example. What are the characteristics of the life together of the members of a neighborhood play, or leisure-time group? Trust in and enjoyment of one another? Extension of opportunities for play to more young persons in the neighborhood? Acts of defiance toward parents or other adults? Achievement of skills—riding a bike, playing baseball, learning about ham-radio operation, building a club house? Getting away from home and roaming around without adult supervision? Killing time at the drug store? Or just gossip?

One more example. What values are represented in the experience of this amateur jazz-combo or chamber-music quartet? Giving themselves and other people pleasure through music? Showing up other people as squares and of low taste? Learning new musical skills and appreciation? Exploring future occupational interests?

If you can remember back to Chapter Three, you can see that all the questions in the examples above are related to a single basic question: What am I here for? And that the answers are suggested in the principles and values and goals set forth in the life and teachings of Jesus. We believe it is God's purpose that all persons shall grow as free and responsible human beings having opportunities for and living abundant lives of work, play, service. Reflecting on God's purpose, we conclude that all groups should in one way or another be in the business of fulfilling that purpose. It will be the basis of the life of the members together, and will form a frame of reference for answering specific questions about the purpose, activities, and values of particular groups.

This basic discipline of evaluating purposes, therefore, requires of every group member that he, with others, assume the responsibility of examining the life of the group to gauge the degree to which it is fulfilling a purpose worthy of persons created in the image of God. Most groups will rack up both some negative and some positive evidences. No group is perfect, and few groups are wholly negative. The task for its members is to sort out which are which when, and to direct the group life so as to increase the positive elements and minimize the negative.

In thinking about your group life, you may also keep in mind that no one spends, or, indeed should spend all his time with other people. Every person requires some time alone when he can cultivate his imagination and renew acquaintance with himself. During these times you may or may not be "busy"; you may be reflecting, or meditating, or dreaming. Some persons need to learn more about how to use solitude, while others need to learn more about how to live in a group. The point is that your life will be richer if you can arrange a kind of rhythm between being alone, doing things by yourself, and being with other people, doing things with a group. How you do this will be affected by whether you live in a crowded household and neighborhood or in a house or locality that provides opportunity for privacy and solitude. Each person must work out his own rhythm depending on his situation and his personal preferences.

THE COMMUNITY OF FAITH

So far we have considered groups organized around kinship, interests, school, skills, hobbies, places of residence, work. There is another group of a different order. This group we call "the community of faith." In a sense it is not a "group" at all, although within the community of faith there are various smaller groups for study, worship, and fellowship. The community of faith should display the highest qualities of community, for its roots are deeper in the lives of persons and its concern is wider and more intensive. This is so because the community of faith deals with eternal values and ultimate meanings. It influences all our other experiences and activities, personal and group.

A community of faith is composed of persons who profess faith in God, have dedicated their lives to him. Together they have a covenant with God that they will be his people and live according to his purpose. Recall the description of the covenant recorded in Genesis between God and Noah as spokesman for his people. These ancient people were a community of faith; today persons associated with a contemporary Jewish temple or synagogue comprise a community of faith; Christians also comprise a community of faith, the symbol of which is the Christian church.* Many long centuries separate the families saved from the flood and the Christian and Jewish communities of our day. During 4,000 years of history much has been learned through God's revelations and the experiences of

---

* Persons who owe allegiance to some other religions also constitute communities of faith. However, their story is outside the scope of this book.

individuals and nations. Much travail and suffering have been endured. The concept and the experience of the community of faith have persisted in human life through all these thousands of years. It provides a certain continuity with the long-ago past.

Today the Jewish community and the Christian community are separate, and there are significant differences between them, especially the revelation of God through Jesus Christ which Christian people view as decisive and as the heart of their community of faith. In spite of this real separation, the two communities share a long history and a vital tradition. They also acknowledge the same values that support community in all group life. They recognize the deep importance of the fellowship and mutual support of those who respond to God's revelation of his purposes.

The life of the community of faith in the Christian view is centered in the worship of God, and includes the study of the content of the faith, especially God's revelation in Jesus Christ, and the carrying out of God's purposes in their daily lives in the world.

In true worship the people of the community acknowledge God's continuing presence, and praise him for his wonderful works and for his constant love and care. They confess their sinful thoughts—those thoughts which defy God and dwell upon themselves and their own desires; they confess their sinful ways—those concrete instances of failure to live as children of God among men, and to act in the light of God's purpose. They hear the word of God preached from the Scripture in its relation to the present world and the condition of human beings today. In true worship members of the community of faith open their minds and hearts to God's Spirit as they reflect upon practical concerns of their individual and group lives, including their life together as a community of faith. They receive forgiveness and guidance from God and rededicate their lives to his purpose. Thus the people celebrate together their life as a community and the faith of each one strengthens the faith of the others.

But the community of faith exists not for itself. It exists to respond to God and to work with him in all the affairs of men, to assume the responsibilities God has given to men for the natural world and for the world of human persons. When the people of the community come together in whole or in part, they worship and study, investigate and plan, conclude and decide, correct and support one another, in order that they may be more faithful children of God in the world.

The community of faith does not break up as the members separate. It continues as the members live in the world. Here they bear witness to the reality and the concern of God as they live out their answers to the kind of questions explored in this book. This includes being more resolute and skillful in building a life in which work, play, and service come together as a response to and as an expression of God's love. It includes expanding the community of faith to include God's people everywhere. It includes extending love to the lonely, sharing food with the hungry, correcting injustice and righting wrongs. It includes being a child of God in all relationships and situations of life.

Thus, you fit into community. As a free and responsible person you grow as a child of God into a full human being in community with other children of God, especially in that community of faith which is your eternal home and which supports and illuminates your life when you are alone and when you are in all the other communities which are part of your life.

PRINTED IN U.S.A.

Are you concerned about your future? Have you problems and conflicts in your family or personal life? Do you find yourself wondering about such questions as "Where Did I Come From?" "What Am I Here For?" "What Will I Become?"

The teen years are the years for asking questions about life's many problems. This book will help you find the answers. It deals with experiences you have probably had yourself in your home, your school, and your community. It shows how through centuries of searching, people have come to find satisfying answers to some of life's basic questions—answers that give meaning and purpose to our lives and help us to face the future with confidence. It deals with the findings of science, of history, and especially of religious faith. It shows how being aware of oneself as a "child of God" can lead to the solution of life's most difficult problems and can contribute to joyous living in today's world.

You will enjoy reading this book, thinking about the questions and answers it presents in relation to your own life. You will find here suggestions that will help give your own life a firmer direction and richer meaning.